Rhetoric – Mastering the Art of Persuasion

From the first steps to a perfect presentation

Horst Hanisch

Idea and text: Horst Hanisch, Bonn

English editing and translation: Guido Michels, Cologne; Jennifer Taylor-Gaida, Cologne

Layout: Guido Lokietek, Aachen; Horst Hanisch, Bonn

Cover: Christian Spatz, engine-productions, Cologne; Horst Hanisch, Bonn

Pictures: Horst Hanisch, Bonn

Publisher: BoD · Books on Demand GmbH, In de Tarpen 42, 22848 Norderstedt, bod@bod.de
Printed: Libri Plureos GmbH, Friedensallee 273, 22763 Hamburg

ISBN: 978-3-7693-1592-9

Rhetoric – Mastering the Art of Persuasion

From the first steps to a perfect presentation

Fore-words ...

in lieu of a fore-word

> *"Man is distinguished by his relatively high intelligence,
> his specialized craft skills and his differentiated language."*
> **Dtv-Atlas Philosophie,
> 9th edition, 2001, page 191**

In the beginning was the word

Or perhaps not? Weren't our ancestors more likely word-less? Didn't the first humans communicate on an unspoken level? After all, a school of fish is able to coordinate its movements without speaking a word. And don't ants communicate non-verbally as well, through body contact? As a matter of fact, language as we know it has only been around for the last 30,000 to 100,000 years.

And even today, we still cannot express everything with words. Or are you able to explain to your neighbour how a banana tastes? Using the word 'banana-like' doesn't count, because if our neighbour had never eaten a banana, this word would still not help him to imagine what one tastes like.

Some statements still demonstrate the bodily feelings language betrays. For example: "I can't stand the smell of him", or "I can't put my finger on it". Sometimes words get stuck in our throats, so to speak.

And, to make things worse, people even tell us now and again that we shouldn't take everything so literally (but how should we take it then?)! Incidentally – some people can't even understand their own words: "I can't understand a thing I'm saying ..."

So it shouldn't come as a surprise to us that, as Albert Mehrabian discovered, only 7% of the information conveyed through interpersonal communication comes from spoken words, while 93% comes from the <u>way</u> in which the words are said as well as the body language of the speaker!

5

Following my standard work on the theme of body language, I will now turn my attention in this book primarily to the topic of the spoken word, exploring <u>verbal</u> communication before an audience. See also my book "Discussion - Mastering the skills of moderation".

Out of the gigantic mass of themes that could be subsumed under the concept of 'rhetoric', I have decided in this book to focus on topical aspects and practical applications. Therefore, the field of 'antique' rhetoric is only touched on briefly as an introduction to the field. I have rounded out the theme by providing excerpts from actual speeches.

The book is divided into several large sections corresponding with the fundamentals of rhetoric, from ancient times to modern usage.

I would like to ask the reader to forgive me if I go into greater detail on some points and sometimes intersperse my comments with humour. In my opinion, it can do no harm when trying to deal with the wealth of material that accompanies us, or perhaps even relentlessly pursues us, day after day, to take out some time to have a laugh.

For example, when I hear sentences like this one: "His wife didn't have time to go to the store, so he decided to run over himself." Wonder if he survived the accident?

Since language obviously does not always follow the rules of logic, situations often arise that summon a smile: Has anyone ever said they wanted to have a word with you (and was it really just one word)? Or did someone once give you their word (did she have only one? - And now she doesn't have any left? - So she is left wordless?).

Well okay, then she might as well tell you "You have my word." (And just where do you have it?). Just recently, someone took me at my word, and I especially like people who hang on my every word, although of course not those who put words in my mouth.

Once in a while, someone offers to put in a good word for me (don't you ever wonder how they decided which word to choose? - Is that why it's sometimes necessary to weigh one's words?).

Some of our peers promise to keep their word (where do they keep it? - clutched tightly in their hand?), while others ask to exchange words with us ("What will you give me for the word "carrot"?).

Others can't get a word in edgewise (why not try it head on?), while the next guy seems to think that mum's the word (Aha – we finally know which one it is!). It seems that a word can be either good or bad: "As good as one's word." (What's so good about it?).

Did you ever hear someone wish they could eat their words? While others were busy mincing their words? Or do you wonder why some folks nod approvingly when words get out of hand, remarking that "those are fighting words"?

Sometimes we are simply at a loss for words. Which makes it seem only logical to me when one spouse says to the other: "The final word has not yet been spoken." Even today, though, I still haven't found out which is actually the final word.

But, wait a minute, I just remembered another neighbour telling me that his wife always has the last word (still don't know which one it is though). "That's my final word!" Aha.

Supposedly, the 50 most-used words in a language account for some 45 percent of any written text. So are we instead impoverished when it comes to words?

In the face of this illogical nature of language, my own views will necessarily dictate the emphasis placed here on certain issues. And it's easy to understand why others may not necessarily always share my priorities.

In addition, some chapters could certainly bear to be fleshed out a bit more. This is why I am always open to constructive criticism and productive suggestions.

Since actions speak louder than words (even good ones?) I don't want to miss the opportunity here to thank all the people who offered me mental and physical support in realizing this project.

I hope you, dear readers, will not only be able to supplement your knowledge of rhetoric, but will also enjoy reading this book and playing with words.

Here's to harnessing the power of language to make the most of your personal and professional future!

Horst Hanisch

Table of Contents

9

10

Chapter 1 – From Rhetoric to Presentation

Rhetoric from Antiquity to the Present

> *"Know thyself."*
> **Inscription at the Oracle of Delphi**

Protagoras and the Sophists

With the end of the Persian Wars, Greece attained great prosperity. People turned their attention to attaining a higher level of education.

In a democratic state, citizens are expected to be able to speak articulately and extemporaneously. Thus was born the 'occupation' of speech trainer.

These peripatetic trainers, who taught elocution and other subjects for money, were collectively termed Sophists, a name derived from the Greek word sophos.

People appearing before court in Athens from about 450 BC could not simply hire a lawyer; they had to defend themselves, which is why elocution and rhetoric skills were in such high demand.

The Rhetor

Originally, the word "rhetor" was used to refer to an eloquent orator who spoke before an audience. Later, the rhetor became a 'teacher of eloquence'.

Previously (see above), the rhetoric teacher was known as a 'sophist', someone who taught rhetoric and related themes for a fee.

There are two disciplines (forms) that are important for rhetoric:

	o the tone and rhythm of speech
• the linguistic forms	o semantics (the science of meaning in language)
	o syntax (sentence structure)

14

	o for example, persuasive argumentation techniques (structures that reveal or conceal the truth). Important here is syllogism, the doctrine of deductive reasoning. A syllogism involves combining two premises to form a third, the conclusion. Example:
• the logical forms	o Major premise: Humans are mortal.
	o Minor premise: Mr. Mertens is human.
	o Conclusion: Thus, Mr. Mertens is mortal.

According to Aristotle, 'human' is the 'middle term' here.

Is Rhetoric an Art?

> *"There are two sides to every question."*
> **Protagoras, a leading Sophist**
> **(around 480 - 410 BC)**

The School of Athens

Raffaello Santi (1483 - 1520), commonly known as "Raphael", was commissioned by Pope Julius II at the age of 25 to paint four walls in the Vatican (the Stanza della Segnatura). One of the frescoes depicted 'The School of Athens', showing great thinkers of antiquity.

At the centre of the picture stand Plato, his finger pointing upward (standing for speculative philosophy), and Aristotle (representing empirical philosophy). Also identifiable in the picture are:

- Socrates (470 - 399 BC) ("I know nothing except the fact of my ignorance.")

- Plato (427 - 347 BC, pupil of Socrates); founded the Academy (Akademos), which was closed in 529 by Emperor Justinian.

- Aristotle (384 - 322 BC, Plato's pupil); opened a school (Lykeion). He is regarded as the founder of logic. Aristotle was the teacher of

- Alexander the Great (356 - 323 BC) until he ascended the throne in 336 BC

Also shown are:

- Pythagoras (580 - 496 BC), the Greek mathematician.

- Heraclitus of Ephesus (about 500 BC), who believed that everything in the world is in flux.

- Diogenes (403 - 324 BC), a cynic who eschewed all worldly goods and (supposedly) lived in a barrel.

- Euclid (about 300 BC), who wrote an influential textbook on geometry.

- Ptolemy (around 90 - 160), who wrote a famous handbook of astronomy.

The Elenctic Examination (Socratic Method)

Socrates (around 470 - 399 BC) realized when talking with his peers that many believed they had a great stock of knowledge at their disposal, but that this often turned out to be only pseudo-knowledge. This superficial brand of knowledge does not stand up to the logic of further questioning. Socrates therefore developed a method, which he called the elenctic examination, to show his partner in dialogue that the latter had not yet attained genuine knowledge, but rather merely pseudo-knowledge.

Pseudo-knowledge

The examination:

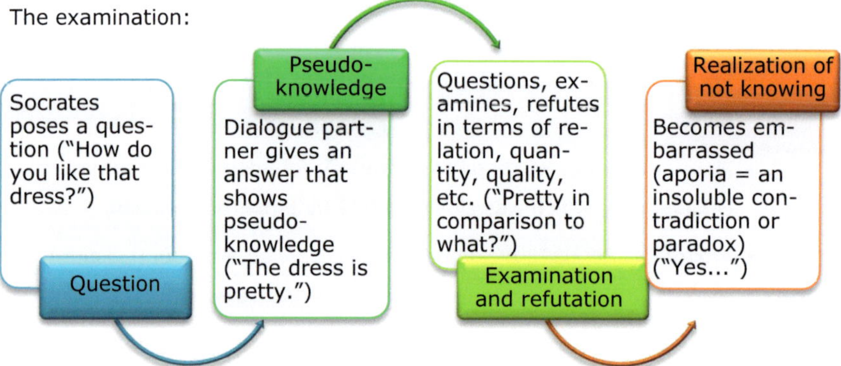

Aporia represents the turning point in the conversation. The dialogue can only continue with a mutual search for practical knowledge.

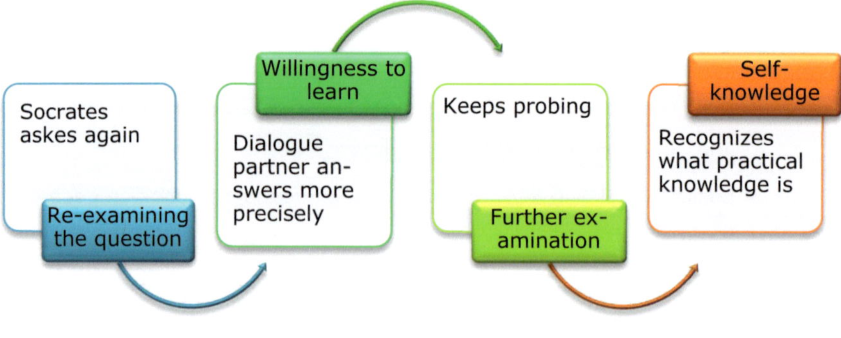

Persuasive presentation

The challenge for the teacher of rhetoric is to persuade listeners of the veracity of any kind of content.

He has to be able to logically present the facts, and even to convince listeners that a weakness is actually a strength. Of course, a sentence might be true in one situation and false in another. For example:

- Major premise: Humans have two legs.

- Minor premise: Mr. Mertens has two legs.

- Conclusion: Mr. Mertens is human.

Or:

- Major premise: Humans have two legs.

- Minor premise: A kangaroo has two legs.

- Conclusion: A kangaroo is human.

From this example we can see that there can be no such thing as objective content. The upshot is the famous 'homo-mensura thesis' of Protagoras:

- "Man is the measure of all things; of what is, that it is, of what is not, that it is not."

The homo-mensura thesis is considered the heart of sophist thinking:

- "The human establishes what is, everything beyond that is rejected (scepticism), and all being is not objective, but rather subjective and changeable (relativism)."

The significance of the Sophists and the Platonic Dialogue

Although in the Greek philosophy of nature man did not play the decisive role, this view gradually evolved into a more anthropocentric one. Man moved to the centre of philosophical patterns of thought.

This is also why verbal - interpersonal - communication, i.e. language, became increasingly important. Spoken language was paramount for the Sophists.

Plato called the drive that always guides humans to the region of true being and the good 'eros'. It arouses in men the longing to devote themselves to contemplating ideas.

In the Symposium this urge is described as the philosophical striving for beauty and knowledge. It takes on a mediating role between the sensual world and the world of the spirit.

In our relationships with others, the pedagogical aspect (epiméleia) of this drive is demonstrated in the way we want others to share in our knowledge.

The Platonic Dialogue

Plato calls this process of sharing our knowledge with others a dialogue.

This dialogue, according to Plato, opens the way for us to remember our past. It works based on words and concepts that summon ideas and memories.

In a dialogue, ideas should be presented logically, i.e. without the help of illustrational tools and images. This is known as dialectics. At the same time, the interrelationships of these ideas should become clear to us.

The participants in a Platonic dialogue thus deliberately take up opposing positions (dialectic = the logic of contradiction), in order to check the cogency of theses by examining their antitheses.

Aristotle and logic

Aristotle lived from 384 to 324 BC. He was a pupil of Plato for over 20 years. In 342 he became the teacher of Alexander the Great.

The syllogism plays an essential role in his teachings. A chain of several related conclusions is one way of providing proof. This method is called deductive, because it progresses from the general to the specific.

In Aristotle's opinion, one of the goals of science should be to compellingly derive what exists from its causes.

The opposite of deduction is induction. Induction searches for common features within a type.

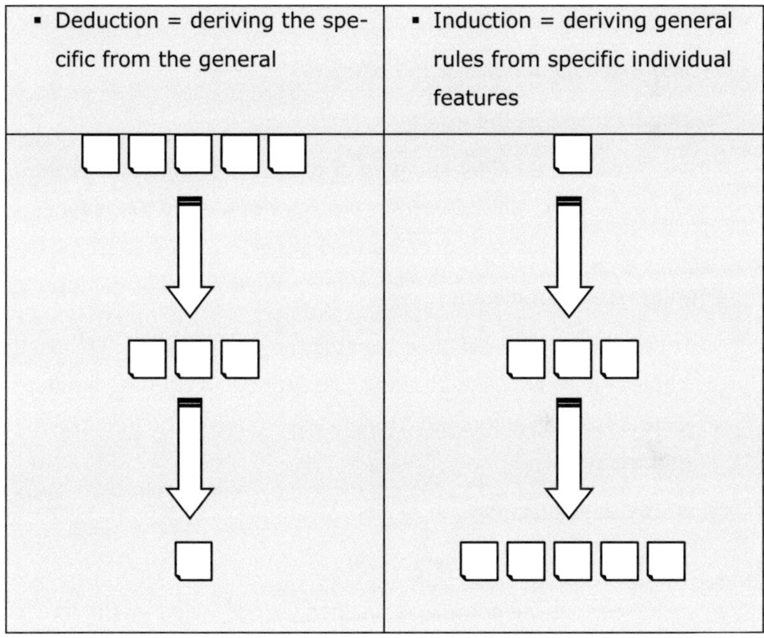

The system of status

Courts of law in particular worked with the system of Status constitutio, dealing with the point that was being contested.

In accordance with Hermagoras, the system is constructed as follows:

Genus rationale (area of argumentation)

- 1st status (status coniecturalis)

    o is the suspicion (who is the perpetrator?)

    o Charge made by the accuser

        - "No" – denial of charge by defendant

- 2nd status (status definitius)

    o is the definition (what is the offence?)

    o Charge made by the accuser

        - "Yes, but a milder category of offence." - Admission by the defendant. However, from the point of view of the defendant, the charge is only justified <u>in part</u>.

- 3rd status (status qualitatis)

    o is the nature of the offence (what is the justification?). We distinguish here between absolute justification (constitutio iuridicialis absoluta) and relative justification (constitutio iuridicialis assumptiva).

    o Absolute justification

        - Charge made by the accuser

        - "Yes, but the crime was justified." - Admission by the defendant. However, from the point of view of the defendant, the offence was justified.

- o Relative justification

  - Charge made by the accuser

  - "Yes, but ..." - Admission by the defendant.

  - Confession (concessio): From the point of view of the defendant, it was a case of not knowing the law or of force majeure, which to his mind justified the crime.

  - Charges are commuted (translatio criminis): The defendant believes that he is the victim. He is convinced of having acted in self-defence, so that he believes the crime was justified.

  - Charges are dismissed (remotio criminis): From the point of view of the defendant, he was just acting on orders, i.e. instructions from a third person. He was unable to – and should not have – acted any differently. He therefore argues that he is innocent.

  - Comparison (comparatio): From the point of view of the defendant, committing the deed was better than not committing it. He had to act as he did. He therefore believes he is innocent.

- 4th status (translatio)

  - o is the commutation (rejection of the charge)

  - o Charge made by the accuser

    - "You don't have the right to accuse me!" The defendant is of the opinion that the accusing body (for example, the court) has no jurisdiction over him.

21

Genus legale (controlling the interpretation of legal texts)

Four categories are distinguished here:

- 1st category (scriptum sententia) wording and meaning

  - o The written word does not correspond with the meaning to be conveyed.

- 2nd category (leges contrariae) contradictory laws

  - o Various laws are played off against one another.

- 3rd category (ambiguitas) ambiguity

  - o Various interpretations are possible of the same legal text.

- 4th category (ratiocinatio) reasoning, conclusion by analogy

  - o There is a legal loophole.

22

Tropes and linguistic ornaments – figures of speech

In antiquity, rhetoric experts distinguished between tropes (locutions) and linguistic ornamentation, and between rhetorical figures of speech in three categories (adding words, omitting words or changing word order) and so forth.

In a trope, one word is exchanged for another, or used to mean something different. In a figure, the word retains its meaning, but other words are added to create a figure of speech.

Since at this point, however, it already becomes difficult to distinguish between the two, for simplicity's sake we will call all of these possibilities figures of speech.

Later on in this book, some examples of figures of speech will be listed.

Constructions

The constructions listed below were important in ancient rhetoric.

Today they <u>can</u> be used, or avoided as the case may be, at the speaker's discretion.

- Arrangement (ordo)
    - o The speech should pick up 'power' as it goes along.
        - "The points addressed should encourage listeners to think about them and challenge them to take action on them."
        - "I see the catastrophe before me, yes, I can even still hear the screams of the afflicted."

- Connection (iunctura)

  - Avoidance of cacophony (the last letter in a word should not be the same as the first letter in the next)

    - "An insightfuL lectureR renderS severaL lessonS successfully ..."

- Rhythm (numerus)

  - Similarly sounding syllables should not be used in the same sentence.

    - "Sally sells seashells by the seashore."

24

Stylization (elocutio)

In ancient times, experts on rhetoric differentiated between four stylistic qualities.

The four stylistic qualities

- 1st category = Hellenism (Greek), Latinism (Roman)

  o use language correctly

- 2nd category = clarity of diction (perspicutitas); descriptiveness (evidentia)

  o build a vivid image (talk in pictures);

  o use a strongly subjective mode of presentation - amplification (amplificatio);

  o get carried away with a topic, for example as a politician

- 3rd category = appropriateness (aptum / decorum)

  o speak as befits the situation (e.g. a funeral vs. an anniversary celebration)

- 4th category = stylistic ornamentation (ornatus)

- originality, build up suspense (instead of: Cleopatra seduced Caesar - The beauty of Cleopatra seduced Caesar)

The four antique styles

Antique rhetoric distinguished between four styles of speaking, depending on the type of speech to be given and the occasion.

- plain style

  o When something should be presented simply. Can be used anytime, conversational tone.

25

- medium style

  - When something is to be set in motion. Makes use of many figures of speech.

  - Is the most frequently used style in everyday life today.

- elevated style

  - When dignified occasions call for careful wording. Best choice of words.

- vehement style

  - When dark passion is to be expressed. Best choice of words.

26

Scholasticism

In the 9th century BC began a period known as the Scholastic Era.

The Emperor Charlemagne (742 - 814) established cathedral and court schools.

The teachers at these schools – and later at the universities as well - were well-versed in the sciences and scholarly disciplines. They were known as scholastics (*schola* = Schule).

Scholasticism refers to the method of examining questions rationally by weighing the pros and cons in order to arrive at a solution. Important features of the scholastic method are drawing on prior learning and the critical analysis of accepted knowledge.

During the High Middle Ages, experts from all disciplines were busy attempting to clarify what had not yet been explained scientifically. The problem was that there were many such specialists, each propagating his own thesis, and some of them doing so quite adamantly.

In order to reach any conclusions, and to clear up the many disputes, discussion forums known as *Disputationes* were set up at the universities.

In these forums, two students well-educated in the subject at hand presented the theses of the opposing authorities in question.

In discourses on the theses, so-called *Quaestiones*, one student tried to disprove the thesis of the other by coming up with an antithesis.

Out of these two theses, or antitheses, a solution had to be found in the course of the morning – the synthesis.

In the afternoon, the *magister*, or master, then presented the synthesis the students had reached to the authorities for their decision.

Even today, this method of finding a solution is still a sure-fire way to untangle confusion!

Thomas Aquinas – Friedrich Hegel and dialectics

Thomas Aquinas, (1225 - 1274), empiricist (empiricism = scientific approach), student of Albertus Magnus.

- For a particular statement, arguments for (pro) and against (sed contra) are sought.

- This is followed by an answer (responsio).

- Finally, the various arguments (ad 1, ad 2; ad 3 …) are examined in terms of the answer.

Georg Wilhelm Friedrich Hegel, German idealist (1770 - 1831), interpreted dialectics (speaking for and against something; the logic of contradiction) as a law that underlies the very nature of thinking and of reality.

In his opinion, every thesis already contains an antithesis. Thesis and antithesis are cancelled out by a synthesis.

Modern Rhetoric

What Does Modern Rhetoric Mean?

> *"Rhetoric is the art of leading men*
> *by the power of speech*
> *to the conclusion desired by the orator."*
> **Theodectes (friend of Aristotle)**
> *(380 - 340 BC)*

The art of speaking

"At German universities, incomprehensibility is cultivated as if it were part of professional ethics.

People are encouraged to display their specialized knowledge using an overblown and inflated style, obscuring banalities behind a dense thicket of academic jargon – the more convoluted, the better."

This is how the chairman of the Association of German-Language Speechwriters (VRdS), doctor of law Thilo von Trotha, inveighs against 'academic hot air.' (Source: Spiegel Online 20 March 2002)

What does rhetoric mean? If we look it up in the dictionary, we can find definitions such as: the study of speaking or writing as a means of communication, the art of speaking or writing effectively, skill in the effective use of speech.

Rhetoric can be divided into the following special uses of speech, among others:

- Theological rhetoric (the sermon); (homiletics = the art of preaching)
- Legal rhetoric (the summation = forensics)
- Academic rhetoric (the lecture)
- Didactic rhetoric (the lesson)

The goals of rhetoric can be represented as:

- making listeners think about a certain topic

- developing in listeners the ability to think for themselves

- strengthening / changing certain behaviours

- reinforcing critical thinking

Unlike communication, in which two speakers convey something to one another both verbally and non-verbally and which usually involves <u>unconscious</u> manipulation, in rhetoric two communication partners try to deliberately influence one another.

We should keep in mind, however, that communication always entails an influence and a potential for manipulation.

Since we constantly communicate with one another (both verbally and non-verbally), it follows that we constantly manipulate each other.

Only by becoming aware of this fact can we try to speak as objectively as possible (i.e. keeping to the facts, free of emotions).

Rhetorical presentation methods

Lady Nancy Astor supposedly once said to Winston Churchill: "If you were my husband, I'd put poison in your tea." Unperturbed, Churchill replied: "If you were my wife, I would drink it."

Rhetorical figures of speech are stylistic tools for elaborating on your point, making it clearer, more vivid and lively. There are innumerable rhetorical methods that can be used to good effect in lectures or presentations. Five groups have been selected here.

- illustrative figures of speech

- insistent figures of speech

- suspense-building figures of speech

- aesthetically illustrative figures of speech

- communicative figures of speech (getting the listeners involved)

31

Illustrative figures of speech

- Cite an example from daily practice.

- Make a comparison with the given problem or challenge.

- Use a metaphor (visual).

- Use a series of images to evoke memories. Make sure to appeal to the five senses.

  o Avoid mixed metaphors: "We are standing on the brink of the abyss – let's go forward."

- Depict an association.

  o for example 'hole' for 'dark'

- Insert a narrative (story).

- Tell an anecdote (can be in first person).

Insistent figures of speech

- Repetition (rouses memories)

  o Manipulated repetition (for example, through careful choice of words)

    - almost 100 people (saying <u>not quite</u> 100 paints a negative picture)

    - as many as 100 people (<u>nearly</u> 100 paints a positive picture)

  o Stereotyped repetition (repeating the same thought in different words)

    - Quote: 'Saying doesn't make it so': William Shakespeare, 1564 - 1616

    - Just because something is repeated again and again it's still not true.

  o Quantitative multiplication (related to number of people)

    - "Hardly anyone objected."

    - "Most are in favour."

    - "Everyone says it's the right thing to do."

  o Qualitative reinforcement (refer to an 'authority')

    - Use media (newspaper).

    - Quote an authority.

    - Cite scientific evidence (tests, studies), statistics.

  o Repeat certain words (as in exclamations).

    - "No one, absolutely no one …"

    - "Then, and only then …"

  o Varied repetitions (same statement in a different guise)

  o Partial repetition (anaphora)

    - "I claim, first, second, …"

- o Extended repetition (geminatio)

  - "I say that we first, I <u>emphatically</u> say that we first …"

- o Repetition of key words in a sentence (epiphora)

- o Compression (summarizing in a few sentences)

- o Exclamation

- o Quote

- o Repetition in reverse order (chiasmus)

  - "Spending money is easy, earning money is hard."

- o Correcting previous words (correctio)

  - "I asked him, no, I <u>demanded</u> of him."

Suspense-building figures of speech

- Escalation (climax)

  - o Temporal escalation

    - "Today … tomorrow … and for the rest of our lives."

    - "First … then … finally."

- Opposite (antithesis)

  - o Pair of opposites:

    - "Love is ideal, marriage real."

    - "To become a father is easy, but to be a father is hard."

  - o Pair of terms:

    - advantages - disadvantages

    - in those days - today

    - intention - result

- o Contrasts:

    - black - white

    - positive - negative

    - individual - everyone

- Chain

  - o One thing builds logically on the next.

    - A because B, B because C

- Reservation - delay (retarding moment)

- Suspense is built up.

- "I'll tell you later one why."

- Surprise (sustentio)

  - o An 'aha moment' is created.

    - "Everyone does it - but not me."

- Announcement (reference to goal)

  - o Here as well, a suspense curve is built up.

    - "You'll be amazed when I show you …"

- Omission (ellipsis)

  - o A train of thought is compressed.

    - "Me … at the market … huge pumpkins …"

Aesthetically illustrative figures of speech

- Seeming contradictions (paradoxes)

    o "Her silence spoke volumes."

    o "No answer is also an answer."

- Glossing over (euphemism)

    o Something is presented as more 'harmless' than it actually is.

        - "letting employees go" = firing

- Plays on words

    o Are tennis players cold-hearted because *love* means *nothing* to them?

    o Is Atheism a non-prophet organization?

    o If you don't pay your exorcist you get repossessed.

- Allusion

    o (Almost) everyone knows what is meant:

        - It was a Catch-22 situation.

        - This was her chance to get her 15 minutes of fame.

    - Similarity (analogy)
        → computer - brain
- Paraphrase

    o "The big guy up there."

    o "In the land of the rising sun."

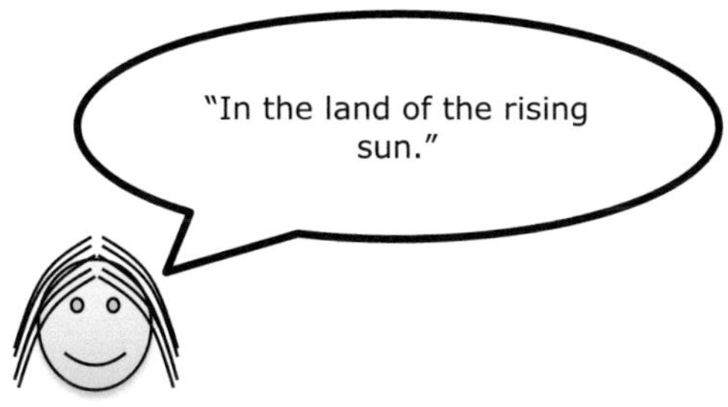

35

- Exaggeration (hyperbola)

  o Builds drama.

  o The exaggeration must be readily discernible.

    ▪ "Millions of people lined the streets …"

- Anthropomorphism, personification

  o A thing is given human characteristics.

    ▪ "The engine coughed and wheezed."

Communicative figures of speech

- Interjection / interweaving of a small aside

- Anticipation of objection (prolepsis)

  o "You may have your doubts."

- Rhetorical question

  o The question could be answered by the listener, but is then an-
    swered by the speaker himself instead.

- A part of something is used to stand for the whole (synecdoche)

  o The listeners know what it's about.

    ▪ London and the USA agree.

Chapter 2 – Stage Fright and Dealing with Stress

Stage Fright

*"A performance without stage fright
is like love without emotions."*
**Udo Jürgens, Austrian composer
(1934 - 2014)**

Nervous before you go on?

It is completely normal and very common for people to get stage fright before they give a presentation.

There is nothing wrong with this - it just shows that what you are about to present is very important to you.

But if stage fright should turn into too much anxiety, it can have a negative effect on your presentation.

This is why it is a good idea to keep nervousness down to a minimum. There are of course many ways to calm your nerves. Let's first take a look at how you can 'mentally' prepare yourself.

The eight cognitive traps

Here is a list of eight traps (cognitive = having to do with cognition, or the mental process of knowing) that you might easily fall into.

Avoid these traps and you can nip your nervousness in the bud.

Trap 1: The black-and-white trap.

This is about 'all or nothing' thinking. This means seeing things only in terms of black or white, right or wrong. Remind yourself of the many shades of grey in between.

"Either I get what I want, or …"

Trap 2: The generalization trap.

We fall into this second trap when we use words like 'always', 'never', 'every', and similar (cf. chapter on 'Generalizations').

"Everyone gets stage fright."

Trap 3: The underestimation trap.

This involves statements that underestimate the value of certain behaviour.

"What I did was nothing special." "It was only …"

Trap 4: The loser trap.

A person who sees himself as a loser, a failure, a flop falls into this trap.

"I'm only a housewife."

Trap 5: The filter trap.

When caught in the filter trap, you only hear the bad things, the negative aspects, getting hung up on problems and focusing only on the difficulties.

"What? Another airplane crash?"

Trap 6: The 'must' trap.

By making statements like: 'You must do this or that', you put yourself under pressure.

"I have to give a talk tomorrow."

Trap 7: The "I told you so" trap.

After the fact, we all know better.

"I could have told you that before." The trap of the 'self-fulfilling prophecy'.

Trap 8: The neighbour trap.

The trap of the guilty conscience.

"What will the neighbours think?"

Dealing with Stress – My knees are shaking …

Stage fright or nervousness before a presentation is nothing unusual.

But if anxiety has a completely negative effect on your presentation, possible leading to a kind of 'Blackout', then it makes sense to find a way to deal with your stress.

Hans Selye (Austrian physician, 1907 - 1982) is so to speak the 'inventor' of the word stress.

But in his theory of stress he viewed the term in the medical context. Today, we use the word stress to cover much more ground and it is commonly understood.

What does stress mean?

Nowadays, we distinguish between eustress and distress.

Eustress

… is the positive, emotionally coloured stress, for example when we are looking forward to a joyful event.

This kind of stress is perceived positively.

Distress

… is a less pleasant feeling, for example in conflict situations, when we have a fight, are under time pressure, etc.

Measurable hecticness

By this we mean the duration of the transient observation, the so-called change of focus.

This is measured by the number of different things the eye fixes on per minute, regardless of which activity is being pursued.

The rapidity of changes in focus has increased significantly in the past twenty years.

This seems to indicate that our brain has adapted to the hectic pace of our performance-oriented way of life.

Year	1975	1985	1995
Changes of focus per minute	226	247	262

Blackouts

Our nerve synapses regulate the overall flow of information through our brains. Acute stress disturbs their functioning.

As the level of the stress hormone adrenaline rises, the synapses are inhibited from passing on impulses. The person affected goes into a panic; he can't think clearly and suffers a blackout.

He can no longer access the information stored in his memory.

Only when the stress subsides can the synapses work again as usual, and the information is once more on call.

What causes stress?

Many people today complain that they are always under time pressure and therefore feel stressed.

We live in fast-paced times, where speed is evidently an important ingredient of success.

While seventy years ago it took a few days for information to travel from one side of the globe to the other, today this can be done in just a few seconds.

We thus have access to far more information than our ancestors. The time we have to react to this flood of information is also shrinking.

"Today in - today out" is the motto in many businesses. "Just in time" is another symptom of how time today is measured in split seconds.

It is therefore no wonder that many workers put time pressure at the top of their list of stress-causers.

Stress might come about due to:

time pressure	high level of responsibility
competitive pressure	necessity to make quick decisions
noise	too much information
poor work atmosphere	mobbing
egotistical driving habits	and much, much more

How does the body react to stress?

Blood circulation accelerates.	The heartbeat increases.
Blood pressure rises.	More adrenaline is released.
The blood vessels change.	Blood is drawn out of the skin, turning the face pale.
Blood reaches the brain more quickly in order to help the person think faster.	The resting tension of the muscles increases, which might cause trembling.
Breath frequency increases.	Digestion is hindered.
Saliva production is reduced.	The mouth becomes dry.
The colon and bladder first demand to be emptied, and then in the actual stress situation stop sending signals.	Sweat (a cold sweat) is produced for better cooling (in primitive situations, during flight).
Pain perception is muted.	The sex drive plummets.

Anti-stress test

The more of the following statements you answer with 'yes', the more susceptible you are to stress.

- I am very ambitious.
- I always want to do things right.
- I don't allow myself to take many breaks.
- I drink lots of coffee to keep on my toes.
- I brood for a long time about mistakes I've made.
- When something doesn't work out, I look for someone to blame.
- I feel sorry for myself when I don't succeed.
- I drink quite a bit of alcohol.
- I take stimulants.
- I smoke a lot to calm myself.
- I frequently react aggressively in traffic.
- I quickly fly off the handle.
- I have trouble sleeping.

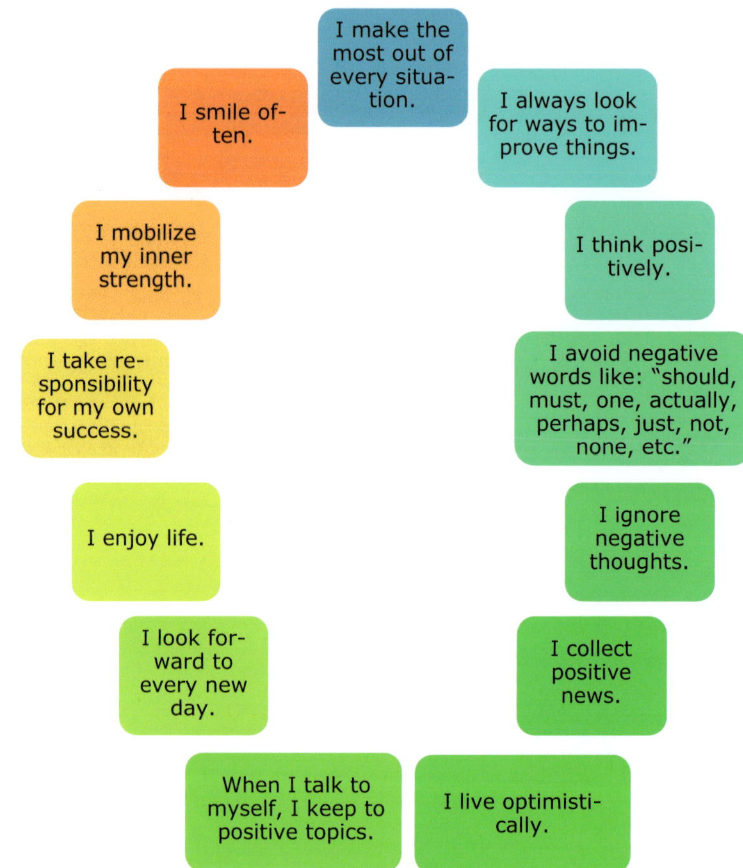
I make the most out of every situation.
I smile often.
I always look for ways to improve things.
I mobilize my inner strength.
I think positively.
I take responsibility for my own success.
I avoid negative words like: "should, must, one, actually, perhaps, just, not, none, etc."
I enjoy life.
I ignore negative thoughts.
I look forward to every new day.
I collect positive news.
When I talk to myself, I keep to positive topics.
I live optimistically.

44

Avoiding stress

Avoid stress situations by:

- Using relaxation techniques.

  o For example: autogenic training, meditation, progressive muscle relaxation, Tai Chi, etc.

- Take a trip to a favourite destination in your imagination.

- Make handling stress a priority.

  o Exchange experiences with colleagues, talk with your partner or friends.

- Mentally prepare yourself to face potentially difficult situations in life.

  o Play out possible behaviours in your head beforehand.

- Try to always distance yourself from what is happening at work.

  o Convince yourself that you do not carry the main responsibility for everything. And above all: Don't take everything personally.

- View difficulties and burdens as challenges to be met instead of seeing everything in a negative light.

  o Strike the word "problem" from your vocabulary and replace it with "challenge" or "opportunity for growth".

- Create a distance between yourself and each stress-provoking situation.

  o Step outside your skin and try to see the situation and your behavioural pattern from 'outside'. Or think about: "What would I advise a good friend to do in this situation?" or "What would a neutral observer say about this situation?".

- Manage your time wisely.

  o Don't take on too much work. Write a list of priorities and decide: "What is really important, what can I delegate or let slide?".

45

- Always consciously take the time to switch off when your work is finished.

- Create a 'stress-free' zone at home.

  o All it takes is a chair where you can switch off and relax.

- Take enough breaks.

  o Retreat to a private room and ask others not to disturb you.

- Deliberately treat yourself to things you enjoy.

  o For example: a delicious meal, listening to your favourite music, reading a good book.

- Turn your usual daily routine on its head.

  o Do things more often that are unexpected and out of the ordinary. This helps you to get away from the everyday grind now and then.

- Try to find a physical activity for mind/body balance.

  o For example: jogging, cycling, hiking, etc.

- Try to develop healthy habits.

  o For example: a nutritious diet, cutting down on alcohol, getting enough sleep, etc.

Chapter 3 – From Greeting to Closing Remarks

Beginning the Presentation

> *"Beginning is the most important part of work."*
> **Plato(n), Greek philosopher**
> **(427 - 348/347 BC)**

Options for beginning a presentation correctly – the introduction

And now the first words are spoken. Is your heart racing? It doesn't matter: here we go! There are several correct ways to start your presentation. We will describe three of them here.

The serious beginning

Would you prefer to start off on a serious note?

- Serious beginning

  - o Begin your presentation as usual with: "Hello … I am … and I will be speaking to you today about … First, let's …"

- Time to think

  - o You present your listeners with a problem. After your greeting, you introduce the problem to be addressed by asking a question: "What would have happened if Cleopatra and Caesar had never met?"

  - o Your listeners give this some thought and are thus drawn into your theme. Curiosity is aroused, suspense built up. You continue: "Hello … My name is … Our topic today is … First, let's …"

- Opener

  - o "Hello … my name is … I've brought you a short film clip." Start your video or film using a beamer (for example, you show three TV commercials).

47

Then stop the device. "You have now watched three commercials. What did you think of them?

- o Then you can directly segue into a discussion. "And that brings us to our topic for today. Namely: 'Does advertising make people stupid?' Let's first ..."

This kind of opener already makes your listeners positively disposed toward you and what you're about to tell them. As a rule, you will succeed in a short amount of time to create a positive atmosphere.

This kind of opener can also be ingenious if you're feeling somewhat unsure of yourself or even self-conscious. Because the attention of your listeners is almost immediately directed away from your person and toward the opener. You are, so to speak, letting others (or something else) work for you.

The hook

A hook can be used to clearly present a situation. Only after the hook do you greet your listeners and begin the 'actual' seminar.

But first you have to find something to grab your listeners' attention, as demonstrated for example in the following.

- Rhetorical question

  - o "Today, we are going to talk about the eating habits of the Europeans. What made us choose this topic? Well, ladies and gentlemen, first of all, let me welcome you ... My name is ... And our topic today is ... First, let's ..."

- Surprise question

  - o "Is there anyone here who would like to eliminate stress from their life?" You can be sure that one or more participants will raise their hands. "You? ... You too? Well, let me first welcome you here today. I am ... and I will be speaking to you today about the topic of 'Fighting Stress'".

- Quote

  - "'We all live under the same sky, but we don't have the same horizons', Konrad Adenauer once said." Your listeners will surely find this amusing. "But first off, let me welcome you … My name is … And our topic today is: 'Can intelligence be measured?'"

- Anecdote

  - "Some say that the graduate with a Science degree asks, 'Why does it work?', the graduate with an Engineering degree asks, 'How does it work?', the graduate with an Accounting degree asks, 'How much will it cost?' and the graduate with a Liberal Arts degree asks, 'Do you want fries with that?'" Your listeners will probably be amused. "Today, ladies and gentlemen, we would like to take a more serious look at the true value of a liberal arts education today. But first allow me to introduce myself. My name is …"

- Comparison

  - "One day, a stout woman came upon a drunken man. 'My God, aren't you ashamed of yourself?' the woman said to him. The drunken man turned and looked at the woman and replied: 'I may be drunk – but you're fat! And tomorrow I'll be sober again, but you'll still be fat!'" Depending on the target group, your listeners may either be amused or horrified. "But now ladies and gentlemen, let me first welcome you … I am … and I will be speaking with you this evening about 'Alcoholism among Youth and Adults!'"

- A true story

  - "When Martin Luther King held his famous speech 'I Have a Dream' on 28 August 1963 before thousands of people, he couldn't have envisioned the world as it is today." Perhaps some listeners will nod their heads. "But before I begin to talk on our topic "Visions Can Come True', let me wish you a warm welcome. I am …"

- A personal experience

  - "While taking the train here today, I witnessed the following: in the compartment opposite I saw an older woman who was obviously annoyed at the behaviour of some young people. They were listening to loud music through their headphones and had to shout at each other to be understood. The woman shook her head and mumbled: 'Impossible, these young people today!'" Some of your listeners will nod their heads in sympathy and others will shake their heads, uncomprehending. "I ask you, ladies and gentlemen: Are young people today really less polite than senior citizens were back in their own youth? Our topic today is: 'Public Conduct in the 21st Century'. My name is … and I would like to thank you all for coming."

Direct launch

Or do you want to jump in 'feet first'?

- "We are facing a difficult decision." The listeners will usually be shocked, taken aback or doubtful.

  - "I would like to thank you for coming on such short notice. Good evening … My name is … and I have to solve the following problem with you here today …"

But not like this! The weak start

- "I'm not really prepared (yet)."

- "Everything has already been said."

- "I would like to agree with the previous speaker."

- "I'm not very good at public speaking."

- "I would like to …"

- "Actually, I wanted today to …"

Bringing in emotions

Here is a small selection of ways to bring exaggerated emotions into play in your presentations or dialogues:

- Ingratiate yourself with your listeners (comprobatio).

- Predict threatening impending events (diabole).

- Express disdain for the arguments of your opponent (diasyrmus).

- Make an emotional appeal (ecphonesis).

- Mock your dialogue partner by exaggeratedly imitating his style of speaking (hypocrisis).

- Complain and moan of your own injury (mempsis).

- Exclaim in wonder (thaumasus).

- Express abhorrence.

Name title and topic? ... Or let the listeners guess?

At some point during the presentation, the title should be named. "At some point?" you might ask.

Yes, and it is common to name the title at the beginning of the presentation.

But it is not a <u>must</u>. Some people begin with a hook or teaser and then name the title. But in general it makes sense to name the title towards the beginning of the presentation so that the listeners know what to expect.

In very rare cases, not naming the title might make the audience that much more attentive and excited, forcing them to listen carefully to find out what it's all about.

For short speeches - usually of the more humorous kind - this might be an acceptable solution.

The goal of the presentation

It should go without saying that you know why you are presenting in the first place.

Which goal are you pursuing in your presentation? Possible goals can be divided into three areas:

Cognitive goals: teaching knowledge and promoting understanding

Affective goals: teaching values and attitudes

Psychomotoric goals: teaching skills

To make sure your listeners don't go home thinking merely that 'it was nice', make sure you are very aware of the goal your presentation should achieve.

Here are some ideas:

- An appeal

    o The listener should take action or buy something, for example in the case of a sales pitch or promotional event.

- Moral

  o The listener should discern a moral.

- Stimulate contemplation

  o The listener should do some deep thinking, take a moment to see something from another side.

- Convey information

  o The listener should have more information at his disposal after the presentation than before.

- Entertainment

  - The listener should be entertained and distracted from his daily cares.

55

Should you put your presentation in a frame?

How do you like the idea of setting your presentation within a framing story? Let's say the title is: 'Marilyn Monroe'.

A frame could take three original forms:

C: (around - the person)	
"Marilyn set off for her appearance at Kennedy's birthday party. In just a few minutes, she would be standing in front of the most powerful man in the USA. And then she saw him ..."	
Now change your physical standpoint (the place you are standing) and your mental standpoint (the person you are representing). Continue in the first person:	
At the end of your portrayal, change your standpoint again and continue with your presentation: 'It must have been one of the most exciting moments in Marilyn Monroe's life.'	

57

A presentation in the first person conveys a course of events in a more tangible, vivid way. The listener can follow what is being related more easily and with greater attentiveness.

A small side effect: in the first person, there is less need to use the distancing pronoun 'one'.

The Main Body – The Security of Structure

Just as if he were taking in a survey, the experienced presenter structures the main body of his presentation carefully.

The main body consists of several blocks set one after the other.

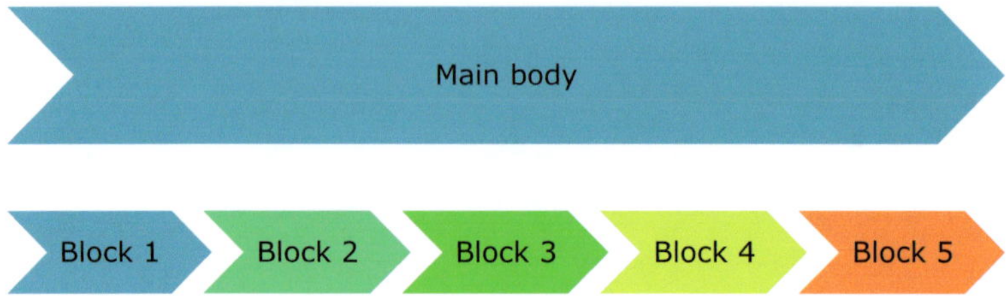

Each block corresponds to a logical unit. This means that the points to be treated in that block are related logically.

> Block 1) General information on dinosaurs
>
> Block 2) Carnivorous dinosaurs
>
> Block 3) Herbivorous dinosaurs
>
> Block 4) Omnivorous dinosaurs
>
> Block 5) The end of the dinosaurs

Arranging these blocks in the right, logically progressing, order is called macro planning.

Within each block the information is once again structured so that each point follows logically from the previous one.

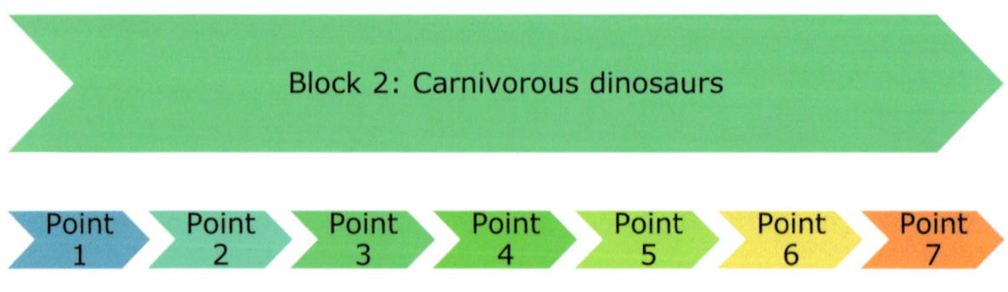

> Point 1: Carnivorous dinosaurs
>
> Point 2: Four-legged carnivorous dinosaurs

> Point 3: Two-legged carnivorous dinosaurs
>
> Point 4: Flying carnivorous dinosaurs
>
> Point 5: Swimming carnivorous dinosaurs
>
> Point 6: Other carnivorous dinosaurs
>
> Point 7: Summary

The order of the points within a block is called micro planning.

Paying close attention to micro- and macro-planning makes your presentation easier for listeners to follow and the structure more readily comprehensible. At the same time, suspense is built up - the listener stays curious and can keep his mind on the subject.

Incidentally: Some trainers think that the main body should account for about 80 to 90% of the presentation (with the introduction and conclusion making up 5 to 10 percent respectively).

Building suspense

The right structure helps listeners to pay attention. Curiosity and the questions each participant is asking in his head, such as: 'I wonder what's coming now', build up noticeable suspense.

Further suspense can be created when the topic is given a skilful psychological spin. We already saw in the chapter on 'Title' that a title with a question mark leaves the outcome of the talk open.

In other words: up until just before the end of the presentation, the listener doesn't necessarily know what conclusion will be reached.

Seven is the magic number

Despite the boundless enthusiasm of the lecturer to impart as much information as possible to his hapless participants, he should nonetheless keep in mind their limited capacity to take it all in at once.

Short-term memory can usually process only five to nine new bits of information on the same material. The average of five to nine is seven.

This is why no more than seven points should be made in the micro planning (see above). The same goes for macro planning: no more than seven macro-blocks.

With the right sub-structure, the 'seven' points can be supplemented (see our example of a presentation on dinosaurs above).

<table>
<tr><td>

- Block 1
    - o Point 1
    - o Point 2
    - o Point 3
  - Sub-point 3.1
  - Sub-point 3.2
  - Sub-point 3.3
  - Point 4
  - Point 5

</td><td>

- Block 2
    - o Point 1
    - o Point 2
  - Sub-point 2.1
  - Sub-point 2.2
  - Point 3
  - Point 4
  - Sub-point 4.1
  - Sub-point 4.2

</td></tr>
</table>

Numbering

People who take a rational approach to their work have an easy time orienting themselves around a numbered structure (first, second, third, …).

Be careful that you don't mention in your introduction that the "following five topics" will be addressed, and then proceed to list four or even six or more points.

The listener will probably be irritated ("Didn't he skip something?" or "I thought that was already the end!").

The structure of the main body

Evidently, structure has a way of giving us a feeling of security. We have something to 'hold onto'.

This goes for both speaker and listeners. So take advantage of this effect: structure not only your complete presentation, but especially the main body!

Incidentally: A logical outline as structure aims at a comprehensible sequence of arguments. And psychological structure appeals to listeners' emotions.

How to proceed through the main body?

Here are some options for how to proceed:

- From detail to big picture
- From big picture to details
- From the general to the specific
- Objectives - planning - execution
- Cause - effect - solution
- Target/performance comparison
- Problem (challenge) - cause - possible solutions

Consider the following possible structures.

Time axis

The time axis is frequently used in the main body of speeches, lectures and presentations.

- Yesterday - today - tomorrow
- Past - present - future
- Grandfather - father – son (in IT data backup)

A tripartite division is already congenial to our way of organizing our thoughts.

And it is easy for many to follow when the main body begins with: "In the old days …" followed by a description of the original thought, the beginning, the vision, the founding, the objectives or something similar.

For many listeners, this answers the question of 'Why?', 'Where did it all start?', or 'How come?'. Then the speaker changes to the present: "Today, the situation is more like this …" and describes the actual state of affairs.

The listener now understands under which aspect the current status should be viewed. And finally comes the third component, namely tomorrow: "How does the future look …?"

The target situation is described. It is now clear to the listeners 'what', 'how' or 'when' something should happen.

Line of reasoning

Here, you work with five blocks:

1. Key idea
   - o Present a key idea.
2. Explanation
   - o Discuss or explain your key idea.
3. Example
   - o Give at least one example for your key idea. The examples should be convincing and optimally chosen to fit the needs of your target group.
4. Conclusion
   - o Derive your conclusions from the examples cited.
5. Proof
   - o Prove through your conclusion that your key idea is right.

Thesis & Co.

Make an allegation: posit a 'thesis', and explain how you arrived at it. In the second block, present the corresponding counter-argument – anti-thesis. Elucidate this anti-thesis in detail.

Thesis and anti-thesis then culminate in the synthesis (bringing together or summarizing individual parts to make a [new] whole, in which a contradictory thesis and anti-thesis form a higher unit). Present your conclusion.

Incidentally: Out of two syntheses you can once again derive a thesis and anti-thesis. And start up a new round of argument.

Pros & Cons

Split your main body into two parts: 'Pros' and 'Cons'. First, explain all the 'Pros' and then all the 'Cons'.

Decide at the end of your presentation for either the 'Pro' or 'Con' side or leave the decision up to your listeners. (Each can for example decide on his own, or you can take a vote.)

Tip: If you want listeners to decide in favour of 'Pro' rather than 'Con', you should list the 'Pros' as the second part of your main body. The reason: what a listener hears last remains in his memory longer.

Advantages and disadvantages

Proceed here just like for Pros & Cons (see above). List all the advantages and then the disadvantages.

Here as well, the second variant should be the one you favour.

Length of time

In your planning, you should establish a certain length of time for your presentation.

Or your client will indicate a specified time frame. For example:

Length of time	Type	where to find
1 min	Presentation of oneself	for example in an Assessment Centre, when the candidate is asked to present himself
2 min	Interview	for example on television
4 min	Persuasive speech	for example, a sales pitch, or interviewing for a job
10 min	Dinner speech	the 'official' protocol dictates how long the speech should be
20 min	Speech	the time will possibly be specified by a client
45 min	Presentation, lecture	for example, specified by a customer or client
> ½ day	Seminar, presen-tation	for example, specified by a customer or client

Even if you practice your presentation at home beforehand and make sure you stay within the time frame, in practice things often turn out as follows:

- The speaker before you exceeds his time slot, so that you have less time for your talk.

- Your nervousness makes you talk much faster than planned. You are 'finished' too early.

- You 'forget' a point and finish before your time is up.

- You get bogged down in details and perhaps have to stop talking before you've reached the conclusion.

- You encounter technical difficulties with the equipment.

In all these cases, you can no longer stick to your carefully planned schedule. This is why it's a good idea in the case of:

In all these cases, you can no longer stick to your carefully planned schedule. This is why it's a good idea in the case of:

- a) too much time

    o to have an extra block in reserve, or

- b) too little time

    o to include a buffer block that can be omitted if needed.

- If a) you are through before the allotted time is up, your listeners or client might have the feeling that they are not getting their money's worth.

    To make sure they don't get this impression, add in a reserve block. This reserve block can be used to expand on the theme or provide further examples.

    Or the reserve block could supplement the theme. But beware: the theme must still be completely coherent without the reserve block! The listener should not notice that you have added in something extra.

- If b) you run out of time, the buffer block is an element of the talk that can be omitted without affecting the cogency of your argument.

  The theme is complete without the buffer block. The buffer block therefore must not contain any fundamental information that would be required for a full understanding of the subject.

  Leaving out the buffer block should not detract from the learning effect in any way. The listener should not notice that a part has been omitted.

No matter which block you use, your presentation should always seem comprehensive and complete to your listeners.

They should not have the impression that you are keeping something from them, nor that they are being 'burdened' with irrelevant material.

66

Active Phases and Learning Units

The human brain can only digest and understand so much data at the same time. If the brain comes 'under fire' from too much information all at once, this 'sensory overload' may cause the listener to switch off. Therefore, people's attention spans are necessarily limited.

After at the latest 20 minutes (!), attentiveness drops to a minimum. This means for you as presenter that longer talks have to contain plenty of variety to hold your viewers' interest. Variety can be brought in through:

- Interaction with the audience
    - asking direct questions
    - asking audience members to do something
    - handing out material to look at
- taking a vote on something
- discussion (for example, following role play)
- active units
- role play
- group work
    - having listeners make something (for example, a collage)
    - having participants present something (for example, the results of their group work)
- brainstorming
- creative interruptions
    - brief exercises for muscle relaxation
    - all participants change seats

Learning units should last a maximum of 45 minutes. At the latest after one hour and 15 minutes, you <u>must</u> give your listeners a break or a change of pace. Otherwise, you risk having them demand a break on their own initiative.

Right after lunch, attention tends to flag because the body is at work digesting. This is when you should definitely insert an active break. Overall, active phases should alternate with passive ones (lectures, monologues, explanations, etc.) during the entire course of the seminar.

If, at the end of the seminar, you hear participants say: "… What? It's already over? I didn't even notice the time passing!" then you can assume that you were able to convey your theme in an exciting way, not least thanks to your careful time planning.

We mentioned the necessity for breaks above. These should be integrated sensibly into the presentation. Not every client likes to hear that breaks are planned (how often? too many? too long?).

On the other hand, breaks sometimes open the way for new and interesting aspects to come to light that can be very welcome in helping to convey the topic. The participants can move around during the break, freeing them from the structure imposed by the seating order.

More reserved participants, who did not speak up in group situations in the seminar room, are more likely to open up in this more casual break situation.

Some lecturers therefore deliberately use a break or two to delve further into their themes. Of course, this is only possible with groups up to a certain size (16 people at the most).

Please don't forget that participants also have other needs to attend to in the breaks. For example:

- washing their hands
- making phone calls
- stretching their legs
- getting some fresh air
- eating or drinking something
- smoking
- and so on …

And finally: Even the most energetic lecturer also needs to take a short break from time to time.

The End of the Presentation – The summary

After successfully getting through the main body, we will now take a look at the last part of the presentation: the conclusion.

It would be a shame - and it would not do your work justice - if you were to simply end with "That's all folks".

The closing section should instead include a short summary of your presentation.

The participant is reminded of the key points made in your talk and the summary gives him an overview - a quick run-through, so to speak.

To make sure the participant's memory is jogged, the summary should recap the points made in chronological order.

Now the participant could theoretically go home. He (hopefully) has more information under his belt than when he arrived.

In order to help our participants get more out of the presentation, we can in the final section utilize one or more of the suggestions made in the chapter on 'The Goal of the Speech', for example:

- Illustrate the results

- Point out a moral

- Make an appeal

- Paint a vision of the future

Illustrate the results

Your presentation should now have arrived at some type of finding. To make sure the participants realize what this finding is, you can illustrate it for them vividly. Especially when you structure your talk (see the chapter on 'Structure') according to 'Pros & Cons' or 'thesis - anti-thesis - synthesis' or similar, a finding must almost necessarily be made.

Likewise, when the title (see the chapter on 'Title') ends with a question mark, your presentation should provide an answer or at least a relevant finding. Even if an unequivocal <u>answer</u> is sometimes impossible with our present state of knowledge ("Why Did the Dinosaurs Die Out?"), you can still come up with a <u>finding</u>. "As we have found, … nothing can yet be proven."

Negotiations can likewise arrive at a finding, even if no agreement has been reached. As the Americans say: "Let's agree to disagree."

And there you have it: since <u>both</u> don't agree, they already have something they can agree on! This means that the partners in the negotiations can take their leave of one another in a friendly and harmonious climate.

That's true diplomacy.

Moral

"And the moral of the story is …"

How many fairy tales and fables end with a moral? A basic truth is illustrated to the reader in a playful manner. And he learns something. He learns that:

- "It doesn't pay to …"

- "It's worthwhile to …:"

- "Even the 'lesser' co-workers, the 'seemingly' weaker parties and others can win if 'outsiders' behave in a certain way."

- "Sometimes, a seemingly hopeless situation or a 'game' that appears to be lost can still be won."

- "For every challenge, for every problem, there is a solution."

Make an appeal

71

"I alone cannot make much of a difference", some people lament. But complaining or moaning will usually not bring the desired results. The person affected has to take action in order to give success a chance, to 'finesse' it.

Sometimes, all that's missing is someone to give that person a kick in the pants. And that's your job as presenter. Metaphorically speaking, of course. Encourage your listeners to take action, keeping in mind Nike's slogan: "Just do it."

c

Visions

Looking toward the future?

Future visions

Was your structure based on 'yesterday - today - tomorrow' or 'past - present - future'?

Isn't this the perfect opportunity to incorporate a (future) vision? Of course, a vision always looks to the future, i.e. it turns our thoughts toward what is to come.

When do we consider a person a visionary? This author believes that what marks someone as a visionary is that he:

- is oriented toward the future

- is regarded as 'crazy'

- is seen as a dreamer

- has flashes of inspiration

- regards his visions positively (at least as a rule, or from <u>his</u> point of view)

- thinks that his visions can be realized universally

- does not pinpoint a certain moment in time as goal

- does not have to achieve his vision in his own lifetime

- attracts followers

- is active in working toward realizing his vision

- invests a great deal of time and perhaps his entire life in achieving his vision

Visionaries – From Leonardo da Vinci to Martin Luther King

According to these considerations, can we count the following figures among the visionaries?

- Abraham Lincoln
- Albert Einstein
- Alexander the Great
- Aristotle
- Caesar
- Catherine the Great
- Charles Darwin
- Charlemagne
- Christopher Columbus
- Cleopatra
- Elizabeth I
- Galileo Galilei
- George Washington
- Homer
- Isaac Newton
- James Watt
- Jeanne d'Arc
- Johannes Gutenberg
- John F. Kennedy
- Leonardo da Vinci
- Ludwig II of Bavaria
- Maria Stuart
- Marie Curie
- Martin Luther King
- Michael Faraday
- Mohandas Karamchand Gandhi
- Napoleon Bonaparte
- Nelson Mandela
- Nicolaus Copernicus
- Sigmund Freud
- Wilhelm Konrad Roentgen

Build a vision into your presentation! Stir up your listeners' enthusiasm for your vision.

Make them so keen, that your vision becomes a goal. How?

Just ask Antoine de Saint-Exupéry, French humanist (1900 - 1944), who wrote in 'The Little Prince' (1943): "If you want to build a ship, don't drum up the men to gather wood, divide the work and give orders. Instead, teach them to yearn for the vast and endless sea.'

Feedback

Now you've finally come to the end of your presentation. Is it really the end? Some presenters use this opportunity to ask their listeners for feedback.

Feedback =

- 1. The listeners express what they observed (perceived) - using an 'I'-statement. "I saw that your language was in line with your body language."

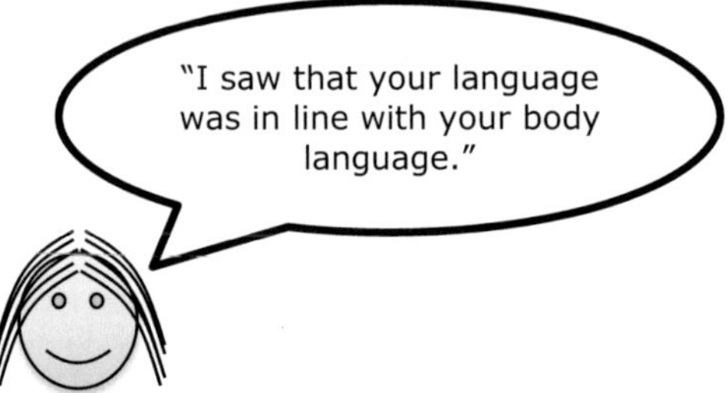

- 2. If desired, the listeners tell what they subjectively thought of the presentation - using an 'I'-statement. "I feel that the examples given were in keeping with my own experience."

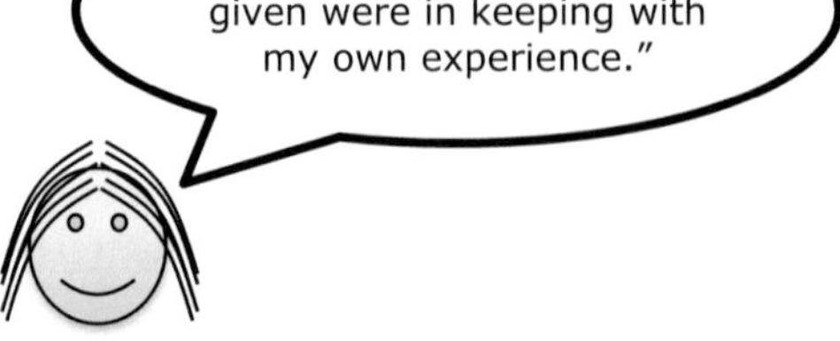

Reversibility of messages

- 'I'-messages are reversible. "I think ..."

- So-called blame messages are irreversible, absolute, such as when a supervisor says to an employee: "You did that poorly."

In order for as little aggression as possible to arise, the feedback should be expressed in a reversible manner. But not every participant is trained to do so.

This is why it's important to remember that, no matter how your participants give you feedback: try to concentrate on what they are saying, not how it is said! The presenter should not immediately respond to the feedback. And he should by no means start trying to defend himself. The feedback is accepted without comment.

It's a matter of politeness to say "thank you" for any kind of feedback. Even if some passages seem critical (negative), you should and must not get angry. Feedback is always valuable for you since it gives you a way to find out what participants think of your style of presenting.

With this information in hand, you can continue to fine-tune your presentations and your approach.

Incidentally: feedback can also be given in written form - for example, with the help of an evaluation sheet. For the presenter, it is always helpful to know what the participants really think.

This is why feedback sheets should be anonymous if possible. Feedback is extraordinarily important for the presenter's further development.

And always keep in mind: Accept feedback with a neutral attitude! Don't forget that every listener or participant:

- has a right to his own opinion

- is entitled to voice this opinion

- sees every situation from his own point of view

- and tries to satisfy his own needs

Discussion

If time has been scheduled for it, you can hold a 'question and answer session' or 'discussion round' following your presentation.

This kind of open discussion gives your participants the best opportunity to clear up anything they have not understood.

It's up to you if this question or discussion session should be part of your presentation. Some presenters conclude their actual presentation with: "Thank you for listening. I would now be happy to answer any questions you may have."

This is a very elegant way of ending your presentation.

Saying Good-Bye / Closing

Whether the presentation is over before or after a round of questions, the presenter must in any case take his leave of his listeners.

An earnestly meant but nonetheless deftly applied psychological element here is to thank participants for attending.

The author prefers the following type of closing: "I would like to thank all of you for your active, constructive participation in this seminar. I am pleased [and you should really and sincerely be pleased - *author*] that you have taken the time, expended the energy and made the effort to be here today.

I hope [and you sincerely hope - *author*] that you have a safe and smooth journey home. Perhaps we will meet again some day. Thank you very much and good-bye."

Follow-up

Even when the presentation or seminar is over, your work is still not done. Now it's time for the follow-up, a chance to iron out any mistakes or inconsistencies for the benefit of later presentations.

Take your time and go through all of the feedback statements or evaluation sheets and suggestions and make a note of what aspects you can improve in the future.

78

Chapter 4 – Speech Training and Presentation Exercises

Speech Training

> *"Improvisation is when nobody notices that you prepared beforehand."*
> **François Truffaut, French filmmaker**
> **(1932 - 1984)**

Practicing speaking

How can you train your speech, lecture and presentation skills?

The best way is of course to practice, practice, practice - in front of an audience.

But who has 10, 50, 100 or even 500 listeners sitting at the ready at home?

That's why you need to make do with 'dry runs'. After gathering your material and giving some thought to what you want to say, try the following:

Mental presentation

Anytime, alone and without my notes, I imagine the situation that I will face as speechmaker. I go through my presentation in my head. This gives me a chance to notice any weak points that I can shore up.

I imagine what kind of objections the listeners might bring up and plan how to react to them. I go through my presentation in my head over and over again.

The goal: By the time my presentation actually takes place, it will be much easier because my mind has already 'lived through' all possible situations.

Practicing alone in front of the mirror

I stand in front of a full-length mirror or a mirror wall and present my
topic. While doing so, I repeatedly
make eye contact with myself.

At the same time, I can check my
body language and how I come
across overall, and critically ap-
praise my eye contact.

Goal: To observe myself and improve any inconsistencies.

Practicing in front of another person

One-on-one presentation for another person
I know who takes over the role of listener.

I pay attention to the proper greeting and
closing and imagine I have an (unknown) audience in front of me.

I don't tell <u>how</u> I'm going to present my
topic, but instead directly <u>present</u> it.

Goal: To obtain feedback from the other person with regard to my behaviour.

But also feedback on whether what I am saying can be understood by
my listeners.

Recording the presentation on cassette

I record my presentation on a cassette.

Goal: When I listen to myself later, I can see if my voice was convincing, comprehensible and loud enough.

Recording the presentation on videotape

I give my talk before the camera. The camera represents my audience.

Goal: When I play back the tape later, I can assess my behaviour and my voice.

Speech and presentation exercises

Reading aloud

Pretend you're a newscaster. Take a newspaper, sit at a desk or table and read the text aloud. Set yourself the goal of repeatedly making eye contact with an (imaginary) listener. Pay attention to punctuation and speaking melody.

Goal: To read from a page but still make eye contact. To comprehend the meaning of phrases at a glance in order to speak fluently, despite looking up from the page frequently.

Content summary

Content summary A (2 - 5 sentences), as close as possible to the original wording

Read a newspaper article or magazine report carefully. Then summarize the content aloud in 2 to 5 sentences - <u>keeping as close a possible to the original wording</u>.

Goal: To be able to recapitulate the key points in a text briefly and correctly.

Content summary B (2 - 5 sentences), in your own words

Read a newspaper article or magazine report carefully. Then summarize the content aloud in 2 to 5 sentences - <u>in your own words</u>.

Goal: To be able to recapitulate the gist of a text briefly and correctly.

Chapter 4 – Speech Training / Presentation Exercises

Thinking on your feet

Thinking on your feet A (choose some keywords and use them in different contexts)

Note down 10 unrelated words. Think up a topic and hold a brief talk using all 10 words in a meaningful way.

Goal: To increase flexibility and realize that random words can be related to each other to create meaning.

Thinking on your feet B

Take a newspaper, open it and put your finger somewhere on the text. Note the word your finger is pointing to.

Count 10 words further and note down that word as your second one; keep going until you have 10 words. Skip any conjunctions (and, or …), articles (the, a, an …), auxiliary verbs (may, can …) and personal pronouns (he, she …).

Hold a brief talk using all 10 words in a meaningful way.

Goal: To increase flexibility and realize that random words can be related to each other to create meaning.

Thinking on your feet C

Choose a word for each of the following categories:

Colours, numbers, famous historical figures, geometric shapes (ball, pyramid …), exotic animals, female first names, unusual adjectives, countries, unusual jobs, foods.

Think up a topic. Hold a brief talk using all 10 words in a meaningful way.

Think up another topic. Hold another talk using the same 10 words.

Repeat this exercise with a third topic.

Goal: To increase flexibility and spontaneity. To discover that a variety of different speeches can be given using the same words.

Thinking on your feet D

Pick 10 very unusual words at random and write them down in the order they occur to you. Don't choose only nouns. And try to select words that are obviously unrelated.

Hold a short speech using these words in the order you have jotted them down. If someone were to listen to your talk, he should not be able to tell that these 10 words were picked out in advance.

He should assume that each of the 10 words is important to the topic and has to be in the speech in order to give it meaning.

Goal: To show that in just a short time a meaningful speech can be given based on specified data and a specified structure.

Narrative

Narrative (your own story) A

Tell (an imaginary listener) a story about something you really experienced. Don't forget to pay attention to logical structure, suspense and a moral. The story should last about 5 minutes.

Goal: To talk about true life experience in an exciting way. The moral is necessary so that the listener can learn something from the story.

Narrative (your own story) B

Tell (an imaginary listener) a fictional story. Don't forget to pay attention to logical structure, suspense and a moral. The story should last about 5 minutes.

Goal: To present something creative or invented in an exciting way. The moral is necessary so that the listener can learn something from the story.

Objective report

Objective report A (summing up an article in one sentence)

Take a newspaper and read an article that is at least one page long. Now summarize this article in three sentences without changing the content. Present this abbreviated version as an objective report.

In the next part of this exercise, reduce the report to two sentences.

And in the third part, only one sentence remains. Don't forget to still convey the meaning of the article.

Goal: To recapitulate complex content in compressed form while sticking to the facts.

Objective report B (expanding on an article by adding your own commentary)

Take a newspaper and read an article that is at least one page long. Now summarize this article in three sentences without changing the content.

Then expand the article by adding your own commentary. Your commentary should include pros and cons. At the end, decide in favour of either pro or con and defend your decision.

Description

Description A

Put a technical device on the table in front of you.

Imagine that you want to tell someone on the phone what the device looks like.

Explain to this imaginary person what the device does and its benefits. You have 3 - 5 minutes to do so.

Goal: To train accuracy and three-dimensional visualization skills.

Description B

Imagine a production process. You want to explain to someone over the phone how this process works. You have 3 - 5 minutes to do so.

Goal: To increase the accuracy with which you are able to explain things. To visualize a process and describe it clearly.

Headline

Headline A

Take a newspaper and pick a headline.

Develop your own (spoken) article for this headline that sounds like it might be found in the newspaper. The talk should comprise about 10 sentences.

Goal: To develop your own ideas based on a given theme.

Headline B

Take a newspaper and pick an article without reading the headline. Develop your own headline for this article - one that might conceivably be found in a newspaper.

Goal: To enhance your quick-wittedness. To learn how to find a fitting, incisive statement describing given content.

Chapter 4 – Speech Training / Presentation Exercises

Impromptu speech (based on catchwords)

Choose one of the titles listed below. Give an impromptu (meaningful) talk on this title. Aim for about 3 minutes.

Why is the world round and not flat? - Why is the cow purple? - What are the advantages of the colour red? - What are the advantages of a ball? - Why flies are called 'flies' - Why are bananas curved and not straight? - Why a sausage has two ends - Why the whale is not a fish - Why does a cow go 'moo'? - What a hole is good for - What makes a clock work - Why a slice of buttered bread always falls butter side down - Why one swallow does not a summer make

Goals: Enhancing spontaneity. Learning to react to the unexpected.

Objective speech

Objective speech A

Choose a topic that interests you personally. The topic should be a factual one (for example, 'The Romans, Wine and the Rhine' or 'Why Did the Dinosaurs Die Out?').

If necessary, note down some key points on a memo card (for example, dates, figures, quotes, etc.).

Stand before an imaginary audience and present your topic for about 10 to 15 minutes.

Goal: To capture your listeners' interest and convey factual knowledge.

Objective speech B

Choose a topic that interests you personally.

The topic should be a factual one (for example, 'Floods and Other Environmental Disasters' or 'Aborigines – How Australia's Native Inhabitants Live').

If necessary, note down some key points on a memo card (for example, dates, figures, quotes, etc.).

Use some visual aids such as a poster, slides or a video clip. Stand before an imaginary audience and present your topic for about 10 to 15 minutes.

Goal: To capture your listeners' interest and convey factual knowledge while properly using a visual medium.

Objective speech C

Choose a topic that interests you personally. The topic should be a factual one (for example, 'The Courtship Display of the Wood Grouse' or 'How Whales Communicate with Each Other').

If necessary, note down some key points on a memo card (for example, dates, figures, quotes, etc.).

Use an audio medium such as a CD, cassette or tape. Stand before an imaginary audience and present your topic for about 10 to 15 minutes.

Goal: To capture your listeners' interest and convey factual knowledge while properly using an audio medium.

Opinion speech / persuasive speech

Opinion speech / persuasive speech A with memo card

Think of an opinion on something that does not necessarily correspond to the majority opinion. Think about how to convince your dialogue partner or listeners that your opinion is right.

Write down a few key points on the topic. Then take a seat opposite an imaginary person and try to convince him of your opinion in 5 minutes. Use the key points you have noted on the memo card.

Goal: Learning how to convince one or more listeners.

Chapter 4 – Speech Training / Presentation Exercises

Opinion speech / persuasive speech B

Think of an opinion on something that does not necessarily correspond to the majority opinion. Think about how to convince your dialogue partner or listeners that your opinion is right.

Write down a few key points on the topic on a memo card. Take a seat opposite an imaginary person and try to convince him of your opinion in 5 minutes. But do <u>not</u> use the memo card during the presentation.

Goal: Learning how to convince one or more listeners without using notes.

Sales pitch

Sales pitch A

Choose a product or service to sell to an imaginary customer.

Set yourself the goal of convincing your customer within 4 minutes.

Think of possible counter-arguments that you can turn into reasons to purchase.

Goal: To sell an idea, product or service persuasively. To awaken enthusiasm, to address the needs of your imaginary customer.

Sales pitch B

Choose a product or service to sell to an actual person playing the role of customer.

Set yourself the goal of convincing your listener within 4 minutes.

Deal with any counter-arguments by turning them into reasons to purchase.

Goal: To sell an idea, product or service persuasively. To awaken enthusiasm, to address the needs of your dialogue partner.

Motivational speech

Motivational speech A

Pretend you're a supervisor and want to motivate your employees. Think up a project to present to them.

For example, 'Changing or Increasing Working Hours' or 'Redesigning Workplaces for Optimal Ergonomics!'.

The motivational speech should last between 10 and 15 minutes. Keep in mind while preparing your talk that your listeners will probably come up with counter-arguments that you should incorporate into your motivational efforts.

Goal: To stir up your employees' enthusiasm for your project.
To motivate your listeners, for example colleagues, supervisors or employees, to take a different attitude to work. Learning to react neutrally to counter-arguments.

Motivational speech in front of a listener B

Pretend you're a supervisor and want to motivate an employee. Think up a project to present to him or her.

For example, 'Taking on an Additional Shift for a Short-Term Project' or 'Postponing Vacation Time To Even Out the Work Schedule'. The motivational speech should last between 10 and 15 minutes.

Keep in mind while preparing your talk that your listener will probably come up with counter-arguments that you should incorporate into your motivational efforts.

Goal: To motivate your dialogue partner and learn how to react to any objections.

To increase enthusiasm and learn how to react sensibly to counter-arguments.

Chapter 4 – Speech Training / Presentation Exercises

Introductory speech

Pretend you have invited a speaker to give a talk on a particular topic. Your listeners are sitting expectantly before you. Your tasks are to:

Open the event - Greet the listeners - Welcome the speaker - Introduce the speaker - Turn over the floor to the speaker - Thank the speaker - Make some closing remarks.

Goal: Learning to open and close an event. Being able to articulately introduce a speaker.

Eulogy

You are standing before the guests at a funeral and need to find some simple and dignified words to say about the deceased.

Goal: To find the right words in a sad situation.

Commemorative speech, keynote speech

You are standing before the guests at a ceremonial occasion and hold an emotional speech lasting 1 to 3 minutes.

Goal: To find the right words in a ceremonial situation.

Anniversary speech

You are standing before the guests at an anniversary celebration and hold an emotional speech lasting 1 to 3 minutes. Proceed for example as follows:

Greeting - Some remarks about the reason for the event - A look back in time - A look forward into the future - Announcement of the next point on the programme or the further proceedings.

Goal: Finding the right words to talk about an anniversary and at the same time pointing to future events.

Toast

Pretend you're standing around with a few guests before an event. You raise your glass of champagne and make a toast to put the guests in a positive mood for what they are about to experience.

Goal: To increase your creativity, originality and spontaneity. To quickly come up with a forward-looking statement.

Wedding address

Pretend you are taking part in a wedding. You have been asked to say a few words about the happy couple.

Goal: In just a few sentences, say something humorous and positive (or perhaps ironic or jokingly negative) about the guests of honour.

Dinner speech

Dinner speech A

You're sitting with guests at a (work) dinner, perhaps on a festive occasion. After the first course, a dinner speech is expected. You tap your wine glass with a piece of silverware to get people's attention, stand up and hold a 1 to 5-minute dinner speech.

Proceed - if you like - as follows: Greeting - Some remarks about the reason for the event - A look back in time - A look forward into the future - Announcement of the next point on the programme or the further proceedings.

Prepare a memo card with some key points to be covered in your dinner speech.

Goal: To convey the content of the speech harmoniously. To underline the importance of the occasion for the (imaginary) guests. To learn how to convey the order of events in just a few minutes.

Dinner speech B

You're sitting with guests at a (work) dinner, perhaps on a festive occasion. After the first course, a dinner speech is expected.

You tap your wine glass with a piece of silverware to get people's attention, stand up and hold a 1 to 5-minute dinner speech.

Proceed - if you like - as follows:

Greeting - Some remarks about the reason for the event - A look back in time - A look forward into the future - Announcement of the next point on the programme or the further proceedings.

Do not use a memo card and try instead to speak extemporaneously.

Tip: Look for an original quote that can be used for many different situations.

Goal: To convey the content of the speech harmoniously. To underline the importance of the occasion for the (imaginary) guests. To learn how to convey the order of events in just a few minutes. Increasing your spontaneity.

Laudatio (speech praising someone)

Pick a famous person. Imagine that this person has received an honour and you have been asked to hold a speech praising this person's accomplishments.  

You can jot down some ideas on a memo card. The speech should last from 1 to 2 minutes.

Goal: To outline the key stations in the life of the guest of honour in just a few minutes.

To ignore any negative episodes in the person's history and concentrate only on the positive aspects.

Acceptance speech

Pretend you have been praised in front of several other people. The others look at you expectantly, waiting for you to say a few words of thanks.

Stand up and hold a small speech accepting the praise (lasting a few seconds or a maximum of one minute).

No aids are allowed here, since you couldn't have known you were going to be praised.

Goal: Increasing your spontaneity. Learning how to react positively when taken by surprise, to say thank you while appearing neither arrogant nor embarrassed.

Small talk

Small talk A

You are invited to an exhibition. Some of the visitors have already arrived. The host introduces you correctly to another guest and leaves the two of you alone.

Make some small talk with this imaginary dialogue partner.

Avoid any themes that might provoke a discussion (with at least two opposing opinions).

Also keep in mind which themes are taboo, such as:

Religion, politics, illness, death, sex, sports

Goal: To learn how to talk with a stranger without preparation over relatively trivial matters. To be able to interrupt the small talk at any time without losing the thread.

Small talk B

You are invited to an exhibition. Some of the visitors have already arrived. The host introduces you correctly to another guest and leaves the two of you alone. Make some small talk with a real person.

Avoid any themes that might provoke a discussion (with at least two opposing opinions).

Goal: To learn how to talk with a stranger without preparation over relatively trivial matters.

To be able to interrupt the small talk at any time without losing the thread. To react directly to the statements made by your dialogue partner.

Interview

Interview in the role of interviewer A

Pretend you are conducting an interview. First put together some questions.

Ask an imaginary person these questions. Include about 8 to 15 questions in your interview.

Goal: To 'entice' your interviewee into revealing interesting and important things about him/herself in a brief amount of time.

Interview in the role of interviewee B

Pretend you have been asked about a topic of your choice by an on-the-street reporter. Think up some questions and give your answers to them in your head.

Goal: To be able to answer questions quickly and meaningfully, perhaps without revealing too much.

Interview in the role of interviewer with dialogue partner C

Write a list of 8 to 15 questions on a topic of your choice. Then ask someone the questions.

Goal: To 'entice" your interviewee into revealing interesting and important things about him/herself in a brief amount of time.

Moderation

You are a moderator and have 5 to 6 guests (employees or family members) sitting together at a table.

Think up a goal that all should work toward together (for example, a holiday destination or cost reductions).

Proceed as follows:

Greeting - Goal of the moderation round - Approach to be taken - Action.

Goal: To coordinate various ideas or routes to a solution and bring them together to meet a realistic goal.

Panel discussion

You are the moderator of a panel discussion.

5 to 6 participants (representing different interest groups) are sitting on chairs in a semi-circle before you.

Choose a topic to talk about.

Goal: To coordinate various ideas or routes to a solution and bring them together to meet a realistic goal while encouraging as much general agreement as possible.

Discussion

You are leading a discussion amongst 2 to 3 participants sitting opposite you.

Half of the participants defend the 'Pro' side and the other half the 'Con' side.

Choose a topic for which people might represent a 'Pro' or 'Con' opinion. A concluding statement is made at the end of the discussion.

Goal: To accept both attitudes.

To make sure all participants make roughly equal contributions to the discussion.

Presentation

Presentation A

Choose a topic. Present your topic in 5 minutes. Use a memo card if you like.

Use at least one audio-visual medium (Smart-board, film, CD, whiteboard or similar).

Pay attention to your body language, eye contact, and a clear and effective structure for your presentation.

Greet your imaginary guests and take your leave of them again at the end of the presentation.

Goal: To present a topic in a captivating way.

Presentation B

Choose a topic. Present your topic in 5 minutes. Use a memo card if you like. Use at least one audio-visual medium (Smartboard, film, CD, whiteboard or similar).

Interact with your imaginary audience. Appeal to their five senses (see Chapter 'Five Senses').

Pay attention to your body language, eye contact, and a clear and effective structure for your presentation.

Greet your imaginary guests and take your leave of them again at the end of the presentation.

Goal: To present a topic in a captivating way.

Presentation C

Choose a topic. Present your topic in about 10 minutes.

Do not use memo cards. Use at least one audio-visual medium (Smartboard, film, CD, whiteboard or similar).

Interact with your imaginary audience. Appeal to their five senses. Pay attention to your body language, eye contact, and a clear and effective structure for your presentation.

Greet your imaginary guests and take your leave of them again at the end of the presentation.

Goal: To be able to grab your listeners' interest when you talk extemporaneously on a topic without the help of memo cards.

Speech training before a test audience

After training on your own, the next step is to practice in front of a test audience.

You can go through the exercises listed above with your audience, each time at five different degrees of difficulty.

First degree of difficulty:

Your audience is seated.

You are also seated.

Second degree of difficulty:

Your audience is seated.

You are standing.

Third degree of difficulty:

Your audience is standing.

You are also standing.

Fourth degree of difficulty:

Your audience is standing.

You are seated.

Fifth degree of difficulty:

Your audience is standing. You are also standing.

Your audience irritates you by un-expectedly disrupting your talk with questions or heckling.

The fifth degree of difficulty should be trained only when you have already mastered the first four.

Explaining precisely

Are you able to explain something clearly and precisely 'without using your hands and feet'? We have as our goal to use gestures in a sensible and persuasive way.

But are you also able, based on the power of your words alone, to convey certain information (as correctly as possible)? Here is an exercise to try:

Sit back-to-back with your audience.

Every listener has a piece of paper, writing board and a pen in hand.

Now try to describe to your listeners what the following drawing looks like using a <u>verbal explanation alone</u>.

Please note: You make no eye contact with your listeners. Your listeners are not allowed to ask questions.

Speak slowly and loud enough to be understood. This exercise might seem easy, but is more difficult than you think.

Try it with other drawings as well if you like.

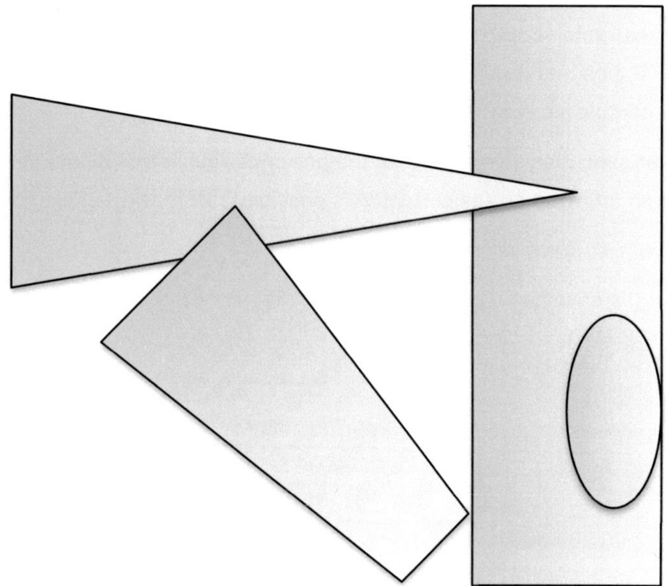

102

As soon as you think you have described the drawing adequately, end the game.

Or explain this picture to someone.

Chapter 5 – Interaction with the Audience

How to Handle Listeners

How to handle passive listeners

After only 20 minutes, listeners' attention wanes significantly. If more than 20 minutes have been planned for a presentation, you as speaker will want to make sure that your talk is as varied as possible.

For example:

- Change your position in the room.

  - Don't stay rooted in place. When the speaker walks back and forth, the listener must turn his gaze and his head along with him. This is good for the work of the brain, because the image on the retina constantly changes.

  - The least effective style of presenting is to remain 'stuck' behind the lectern two hours long. As already mentioned above, walking back and forth should be done in moderation, in order to avoid the kind of 'hyperactivity' that will only make viewers nervous.

  - Incidentally, some presenters even walk through the audience briefly.

- Use attention-getting gestures.

  - Pay attention to body language (see the book 'Body Language in Europe' by the same author). Use your body. Show that you are 'alive' and that your theme is 'lively' and interesting.

- Use media.

  - o Integrating media into your talk helps to maintain listeners' attention span.

- Add variety.

  - o As described in the chapter on 'Active Phases', a variety of activities offered by the presenter can be used to pique listeners' interest and hence increase their attentiveness.

- Address the listeners.

  - o Address your listeners by interacting with them or directly asking them questions. This pulls the passive listener out of his lethargy (listlessness, idleness). Since other listeners will now 'fear' that they're next, they will pay more attention to what is going on.

- Bring some 'colour' into your presentation.

  - o This means: don't act and speak in dry, monotonous tones, 'colourlessly', but instead find ways to stir things up a little.

  - o For one thing, through the use of gestures and appropriate facial expressions, and for another by painting vivid pictures, using multiple adjectives, visualizing what you're talking about. Make your presentation a lively and colourful one. Your audience will thank you by paying more attention.

- Maintain eye contact with the audience.

  - o Show your audience again and again that you do not view them as an anonymous sea of faces. Try to look at each listener directly at least once. With a large audience, this might seem almost impossible. But you can still cast your eyes across all areas where people are sitting. Each listener will then have the subjective perception of having been acknowledged.

How to handle active listeners

There are some listeners who will try to take very active part in your presentation.

They might interrupt you with questions or remarks, rustle around with their own papers, or exchange comments with their neighbours.

The presenter should under no circumstances simply ignore such behaviour, because this situation can otherwise quickly lead to the emergence of an 'oppositional participant'.

That's why it's best to:

- look at the person

- nod at him

- and, if appropriate, address him.

Listener interaction

By interaction we mean an active exchange between listeners and presenter. Interaction brings the listener into action.

Listeners don't only passively sit there and absorb what you're saying, they also have their own thoughts on what's being said. To define them as purely passive listeners does not do them justice.

Listeners also watch what is happening before them. So they can also be regarded as viewers. Since the brain is called into play during the presentation, they are also co-thinkers.

Let your listeners actively share their thoughts. Integrate them into your presentation. Get interactive!

- The listener will feel acknowledged and taken seriously.

- With his reactions, he will influence the further course of the presentation.

- Playing an active role increases his suspense and curiosity, in turn leading to greater attentiveness.

- Since he has been permitted to have an influence on how the presentation goes, he will tend to agree with your statements.

- His level of satisfaction rises, so that at the end of the presentation, he will return home happy with what he has experienced.

But what's the best way to get interactive? There are several options:

- Shaking each participant's hand

- Asking a rhetorical question

- Posing an actual question to a participant, such as:

  o "Do you think that …?"

  o "Do you also think that …?"

- Asking people to raise their hands

  o "Who among you thinks that …?"

- By taking a vote. The listeners are asked for their opinion.

  o "Who among you is in favour of … - Please raise your hand!"

    - The results of the vote can perhaps be used later, for example to illustrate how the participants' viewpoints have changed during the presentation.

- You can create a statistic based on the results of the vote.

  o "The results of our vote here are similar to those obtained in a survey …"

  o "As we can clearly see, most of us …"

    - Of course, votes can also be conducted by closed ballot.

- By distributing visual aids. Suspense is built up, and some variety brought in.

  o "Please take a look at the … that is being passed out."

    - With a visual aid in hand, the participants are able to better 'grasp' the material.

    - Such visual aids can even be given a certain smell.

- Please keep in mind, however, that as soon as you hand something out, participants' attention will be devoted to examining the material they are holding. This will distract their attention from you for a while. On the other hand, you have managed in this way to stimulate one or more of their senses. If you go so far as to offer a taste sample: "Just try … for yourself", the sense of taste will also be actively stimulated.

108

- By asking for help
  - "Would you please hold this for a moment, so that I can …"
- By having them write something down
  - "Please write down the …"
- By role play, group work, or similar.

Role Play and Other Active Components – but very respectable ones

Many kinds of learning can be better conveyed by means of group work, exercises, games or role play.

And besides the greater learning effect, it is more interesting for (most) participants to take an active part in the event.

The 'experiential' component is important here, because 'experience' cannot be 'taught', but must be lived.

It's always important to tell participants:

- what the point of the exercise is

- who is supposed to do what

- how much time is allotted

And don't forget: never expose anyone to ridicule!

109

Exercises

Conducting an exercise.

- Set a task

  o clearly

  o in as few words as pos-
    sible

  o with precisely defined
    terms

  o comprehensibly

  o if appropriate, in writing

- There must be a readily discernible connection with actual practice.

- The exercise

  o brings some variety to the talk

  o creates an active phase

  o let each person play an active part

  o motivates the participants

  o must not overtax the participants

o fits in with the material to be learnt

Assessment

- The participants present their results

    o possible exchange of thoughts and discussion

- summary by the presenter

Seat your participants in such a way that they can all see well.

110

Group work

Conducting group work:

- Set a task

    o discuss what is to be accomplished

    o name an exact topic and goal

    o define a precise time frame

    o if appropriate, divide the task into several sub-tasks (for different groups)

    o if needed, distribute work materials

- assign rooms for each group

- Form groups based on

    o identical themes

    o different (sub) tasks

- Working in the groups

- allotted time is specified

- groups should not disrupt each other's work (acoustically)

- the group itself defines how exactly to proceed within the group

- the group selects a group speaker

- Summary

    o the groups summarize their results

- Presentation of results

- the groups present their results to the others

- Sharing and discussion

    o the groups share what they have learned, declare and back up
      their opinions

- Summary by the presenter

The listener emphatically (aggressively) supports a different view

A listener is disrupting you? You have the feeling like he wants to provoke you? This is a risk you should not underestimate. You need to ensure you keep a tight hold on the reins and to maintain your authenticity. Some advice on how to act in this type of situation is as follows:

- stay calm

- signal non-verbal acknowledgement

  o nod to him, smile at him.

- answer in short sentences

  o "Yes, but ..."

- avoid provocation

  o "That is an interesting view, but ..."

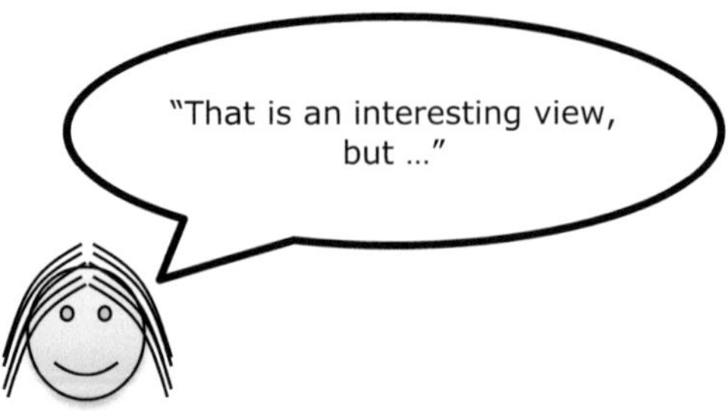

- Include a question in your answer

    o He who asks, leads

- ask your counterpart to clarify his understanding

    o "What is <u>your</u> understanding ...?"

- Hold direct eye-contact. Look clearly into the eyes of the other person in order to demonstrate your strength.

- raise and identify the mistakes in the other person's point

- at the same time, look for similarities

- during the dialog, try to put yourself into the other person's place:

    o actively perceive his views

- you also can intentionally misunderstand the verbal attacks of your conversation partner or use them in another sense

- end the dialog with a consensual agreement

    o "We agree that we don't agree"

- postpone a deeper discussion to the end of the presentation or to the next break

    o "I'd like to clear that point with you in our next break."

To reply to an objection

You have several different possibilities to reply to an objection.

- further inquiry method
    - wins some time
    - rephrase the objection into a question in order to gain time. "Your question is ..."
- reserve method
    - respond later. "I'm happy to answer that in our next break." (Or at the end of the speech)
- presumption method
    - prevent an objection. "You may state that ... but ..."
- yes, but method.
    - "Yes, that's correct, and therefore ..."

- advantage-disadvantage method
    - acknowledge disadvantages, but accentuate advantages. "The disadvantage is ..., but here, the advantage prevails ..."
- distraction method
    - bring different views into the discussion

- divisions method

  - amount or group divided by the information you have, for example. "10,000? We are talking about 80 million Germans, so that is only 0.000125 %."

- multiplication method

  - information is multiplied with the amount or group, for example. "Every fifth one? We are talking about 1 million inhabitants in Cologne, which means a total of already 200,000 people!"

- boomerang method

  - turn an alleged disadvantage into an advantage

- transformation method

  - repeat objection in an interrogative form in order to transform it into a positive objection

- display method

  - the person always finds a counter-argument. "Under which circumstances would you …"

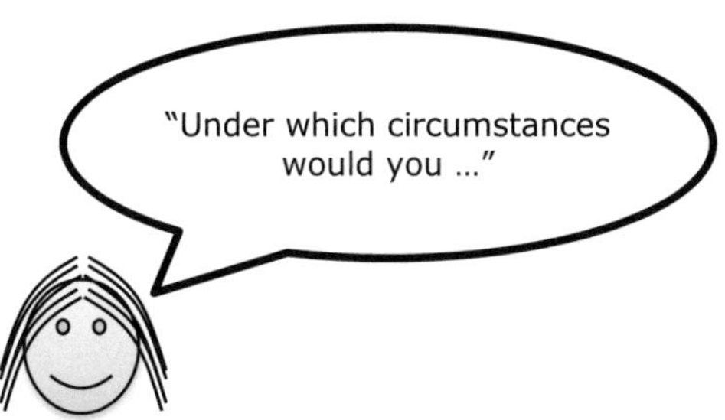

What is the purpose of the discussion?

The purpose of most conversations is to persuade somebody else.

Before a discussion you should think about why you are talking with each other. The other person should have the feeling that he

- can gain new knowledge,

- can influence your viewpoint,

- can persuade the you to agree with his own idea,

- can exchange experiences with like-minded people,

- can reach an ambitious aim,

- and much more.

Define for yourself the purpose of a discussion before it starts: "What do I want to get out of it?"

Chapter 6 – Speaking with Your Body – Body Language

The Basic Vocabulary of Body Language

> *"The rest is silence."*
> **William Shakespeare, English writer**
> **(1564 - 1616)**

Language and body language: the 7/93 rule

You've prepared well, practiced your presentation several times, polished every word and sentence for 'hours'. Your presentation is 'complete'.

And now it's time to get up and address your public. After just a few minutes, you notice that the attention of a few listeners seems to be waning.

One looks at his watch, the other yawns widely. And what's this? The third person seems to be dropping off.

Irritated, you lose your thread. You get nervous. The end of your presentation is greeted with unenthusiastic applause.

What went wrong? Maybe you just never heard of the '7/93 rule'? It states that, of 100% information conveyed

- only 7% relates to the spoken word and

- as much as 38% has to do with <u>how</u> words are said (voice - melody - tone, monotony, etc.) and

- and an astounding 55% can be traced to body language!

(according to a study by Albert Mehrabian, [*1939])

55% - that's more than half! - is expressed by the language of the body (non-verbally), and only 7% by the actual words (verbally)!

Are you surprised, astonished or perhaps simply can't believe this finding? Please think for a moment about the implications:

- It (almost) doesn't matter, <u>what</u> we say, but rather

- <u>how</u> we say it.

The whole 'trappings' surrounding the talk also influence our listeners.

It's no wonder then that some shareholder meetings and company presentations sometimes turn into flashy shows.

We evidently live in times when people are longing for 'adventure', as in:

- adventure restaurants

- adventure travel

- adventure shopping, and the inevitable

- adventure presentation

The line between presentation and show is hard to draw.

You have to decide for yourself how much adventure to build into your presentation. Perhaps you would consider the ratio 7/93?

The ABC's of body language with regard to ...

... *your own outward appearance*

Not only the body speaks to us, but also its 'outfit'.

- Clothing
    - modern, conservative, dirty …
- Scent
    - obtrusive or subtly accentuating the personality …
- Status symbols
    - car, special seating …
- Accessories
    - briefcase, pens …
- Jewellery
    - eyeglasses, watch …

... *the audience and the room*

- Levels
    - hierarchy
    - intellectual level
    - language
    - communication
- Territories
    - in the boss's office or
    - in the cafeteria
- Location
    - behind a lectern or
    - freestanding

119

- Choice of seat

  o with back to the window

  o or to the door

- Space cushion (distance zones)

  o 0 - 50 cm

    - Intimate. Exceptions in the case of hairdresser, dancing, etc.

  o 50 - 100 cm

    - Personal distance, for example when engaged in small talk.

  o 100 - 200/300 cm

    - Social distance, waiting zone, for example when someone has entered a room.

  o more than 200/300 cm

    - Public distance, for example when a speaker talks to an audience.

... *your own body position*

- posture

- gait

- gestures

- facial expression

- breathing

- voice, tone, speaking

- rhythm

Gestures – When speaking

Some speakers want to captivate the audience with their words, but they stand there as if rooted to the ground, like a 200-year-old oak tree.

The longer a presentation lasts, the more monotonous and boring such a speaker will seem to his listeners.

By contrast, other speakers jump back and forth across the stage as if pursued by a swarm of hornets. This makes the presentation seem agitated and confusing to the listeners.

Something in between these two extremes seems appropriate for most talks. In order to use gestures effectively, the presenter should be able to move freely.

This means that he should be neither 'chained in place' (for example, behind a lectern) nor hampered by his clothing. This is why 'dressing to impress' is important.

- The clothing should fit the occasion for the talk.

- It should fit the theme of the talk.

- The audience should not be distracted by speaker's outfit, but should instead be able to concentrate on the content of the presentation.

Dress should be suitable for the target group as well as for the occasion. To make sure you show yourself from your best side, you should feel comfortable in the clothes you are wearing.

Clothing that is too tight, or sleeves that slide up almost to your elbows when you raise your arms will hinder the targeted use of gestures.

Likewise, if you tend to perspire a lot and might be self-conscious about sweat marks under your arms, this might inhibit you from gesturing freely.

Let's take a look at arm position. Using your arms well can support your arguments. Careful: don't cross your arms in front of your chest, especially at the beginning of your presentation.

The arms should not be closed in front of the body, since this position might be read as a 'blockade'.

Arms crossed in front of the chest

This posture is usually read negatively as a reaction to something that has happened.

The person is closing himself; perhaps he is scared, inhibited or uneasy and is trying out of fear to defend himself against a perceived attack.

Hands on hips

The speaker is trying to make himself bigger and stronger than he is. At the same time, he is holding onto himself for stability.

This posture is trying to put up a brave front, and also expresses indignation: "Well, just let me tell you something!"

Holding the lower arm with the opposite hand

A certain insecurity is perceptible.

The speaker is hiding behind his own arms.

Pleading pose

The fingers are intertwined: "Please don't hurt me."

"Don't ask me any questions that I can't answer."

This gesture does not necessarily show strength.

One hand in the pocket

This is supposed to look casual.

It is permissible according to today's etiquette, but only now and again, and not in the first few minutes.

This pose looks slightly arrogant to the audience.

Two hands in the pockets

Current manners view this pose as very impolite and arrogant.

The person is trying to show that he's in control of the situation, but the truth is that he's probably very nervous.

Hands behind the back

The hands are hidden from the audience. This prevents the listeners from being able to read gestures.

It's meant to convey: "I'm behaving myself and listening attentively." But if overdone this posture seems too submissive and 'weak'.

One arm bent

One arm is bent and the hand held before the abdomen.

This is seen as a slightly protective pose and doesn't make a very good impression on listeners.

123

Begin your presentation (with the appropriate gestures) only when you <u>and</u> the audience are ready.

Give your listeners some time to settle down.

Arms close to the body

Closely controlled arm movements while speaking and gesticulating reveal a certain amount of insecurity.

The arms are kept close to the body, ready to defend it in case of attack.

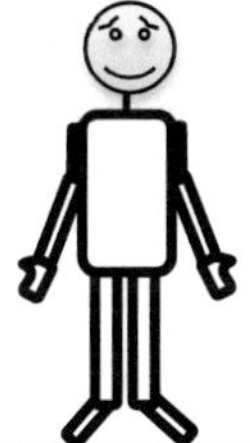

Arms reaching forward

By reaching forward, the person shortens the distance to his dialogue partner. This is seen positively.

This posture says: "I warmly welcome you." Or: "Come to me."

Fingers form a pointed 'roof'

If the fingertips point upward to form a pointed roof, this might convey arrogance: "Listen to me!"

If the fingertips point towards the person opposite, a verbal attack can be expected.

Pay close attention in particular to the position of your hands.

Don't make a fist or stretch your fingers out stiffly (better is a relaxed hand = acceptance and offering).

We can express a great deal with our fingers and hands, including with a hand curled into a fist.

Of course, this also opens the way for misunderstandings, which is why you should be careful with hand motions of any kind. But don't let fear stop you from making any gestures at all, or else you could forfeit your innate human power of expression.

Rubbing the hands

The person is self-confident and in a good mood. He believes the deal is 'signed and sealed'.

A typical gesture by salespeople who have closed a sale.

This hand gesture is usually reinforced by a positive facial expression, such as a mischievous smile.

Paving the way with one hand

The person uses this hand gesture to make his way through an imaginary crowd.

This is done to clear some space to get through, or in the presentation to 'plough through' the arguments that have been launched.

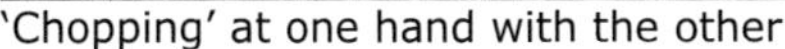

'Chopping' at one hand with the other

This is an aggressive gesture. An objection is being 'chopped off' and the argument 'chopped up'.

This gesture might be saying: "Let's get things straight.";
"This is what I mean and nothing more." The person wants to cut off any further discussion on the topic.

In general, approving gestures lead upward toward the body and disapproving ones downward and away from the body.

And grand gestures seem exaggerated while smaller ones seem more modest.

125

As in so many things, the 'golden mean' seems the best way to go in our latitudes.

Involuntary and voluntary gestures

We can distinguish between involuntary and voluntary gestures.

The first group includes inborn reflexes (protective reflexes), which our body uses 'in defence'. These prevent, for example, a fly from flying into our eye (at least most of the time).

There are also learned reflexes, such as spontaneous ducking by someone who was often hit on the back of a head as a child.

The second group consists of voluntary gestures. These are movements of the head, arms and hands that are made deliberately:

Underlining gestures

Cuts something, chops off

Emphasizing gestures
Underpinning the statement made

Delimiting gestures
Define the space

Signing to replace spoken language
Sign language

Illustrating gestures
Painting characters in the air

Symbolic gestures

OK sign, etc.

Touching gestures

Touching the dialogue partner grabs his attention

Pointing/indicating gestures

Draws attention. Left hand = feelings, right hand = objective interest

Demonstrative gestures

Showing sizes and dimensions

Eye contact

*"He who can no longer pause to wonder
and stand rapt in awe,
is as good as dead; his eyes are closed."*
**Albert Einstein, German physicist
(1879 - 1955)**

Look me in the eye ...

People often say that the eyes are the windows to the soul. Is this really true? Well, the eyes certainly reveal a great deal. They can shine or they can seem dead. They can look inquisitive, bore into us, seem remote and dreamy, in love, flashing with evil ...

The pupils may be either small or dilated, the eyes narrowed to slits or wide open. If eye contact is maintained by our dialogue partner, we assume he is open and attentive.

Eyes cast downward signalize inhibition, shyness, sadness or even an attempt to swindle. "He's unable to look me in the eye."

If your gaze remains fixed for too long on your partner, however, he will feel uneasy. We get nervous or even aggressive if someone looks at us too intently.

It makes us feel like the other guy is stronger than us, trying to stare us down. As a presenter, this means that you should try to make eye contact with all participants now and again without however staring at them.

Incidentally: According to Doreen Kimura, a Canadian psychologist, when a man and a woman meet for the first time, it is the woman who seeks eye contact more actively.

The woman tries to draw out the man, as exhibited by her gestures and facial expressions. Only based on these triggers does the man then take an active part in the conversation.

When the woman is ovulating, her verbal capabilities reach a high point.

The Duchenne Smile – The 'true' smile

As early as 1862, the French anatomist Duchenne already noted the barely perceptible difference between the truly joyous smile and the grimace-like grin.

Duchenne established that a smile with the mouth is not a sign of cheerfulness until the muscles surrounding the eyes also contract.

The so-called 'Duchenne smile' is regarded today as an expression of open and untroubled good cheer.

More than 100 years later, in the 1970s, Paul Ekmann noticed in a study of facial expressions that exactly 24 facial muscles work together to reflect the whole spectrum of possible emotions when we feel superior or inferior.

This interplay of the facial musculature says much more than spoken words can, even revealing who has the upper hand when two people are engaged in a dialogue.

According to Jörg Metren, a psychologist at the University of Saarbrücken, the facial muscles signalize for a split second an almost unconsciously perceptible expression of disgust when a person is stared at for too long.

The upper lip curls upward and the nostrils draw in slightly.

In 1978, Carl-Herman Hjortsjö and Ekmann introduced the concept of 'action units'. According to these two researchers, the elementary facial movements can be categorized according to 46 of these so-called 'action units'.

The complete range of facial expressions is made up of these basic units.

For example:

- 'Action Unit 12' ('raising the corners of the mouth')
- 'Action Unit 6' ('raising the cheeks')

The human smile is characterized by a fixed sequence of muscle movements. This sequence shows whether it is a true smile.

If the smile is faked, the sequence is delayed or changed. After decoding these movement sequences, Terrence J. Sejnowski launched an interesting series of experiments.

He succeeded at programming a computer to tell a fake smile from a genuine one 95% of the time. The goal of this computer project is to decode all of the information that the face involuntarily and unconsciously conveys.

As a vision that could become reality in the not-too-distant future, this system could be used to successfully identify people and then authorize/give them access to accounts, safes, entry gates, etc.

It could help physicians, psychiatrists and psychologists to interpret the facial expressions of their patients. Undreamt-of possibilities open up for legal proceedings or police interrogations.

Passport control could take a new form, bank robbers would be easier to identify; in dialogues, negotiations and sales pitches, it would be much harder to keep secrets.

The down side, however, is that absolute surveillance, and not only in cities, would no longer be a utopian vision.

The biometric surveillance system

(from the *Generalanzeiger Bonn* newspaper, 12 July 2001):

'The guest … was enjoying a beer when three policemen suddenly appeared and arrested him … 36 cameras are mounted in the district to keep watch over all passers-by and to compare their facial features with the photos of tens of thousands of criminals using biometric software.'

Biometric systems utilize certain body traits to identify an authorized user and allow him to log in. This might be done by means of fingerprint, voice or the iris of the eye. Are we soon to experience total state control?

Basic Emotions – From joy to sadness

Wallace Friesen found out that the same, typical facial muscles always come into play when small children feel fear, disgust, anger, surprise, joy and sadness; later, shame and contempt are also expressed by the same muscles every time.

If a person (unconsciously) experiences one of these basic emotions, the corresponding facial muscles are activated and the matching 'action units' come into play. For:

Joy

- raising the cheeks

- raising the corners of the mouth

- opening the lips

Sadness

- raising the root of the nose

- lowering the eyebrows

- lowering the corners of the mouth

Surprise

- raising the root of the nose

- raising the corners of the eyes

- raising the eyelids

- lowering the lower jaw

Anger

- lowering the eyebrows

- raising the eyelids

- tightening the eyelids

- pursing the lips

Fear

- raising the root of the nose

- raising the corners of the eyes

- lowering the eyebrows

- raising the eyelids

- spreading the lips

- opening the lips

Disgust

- raising the upper lip

- furrowing the chin

- lowering the eyebrows

- wrinkling the nose

- jutting the lower lip out

Does body language lie?

We recognize that body language existed long before the spoken word. Therefore, reactions inside our body and with our body are automatic, excitable, and unconscious.

Research has verified that certain reactions are the same all over the world and that they are also interpreted the same!

We can expect that body language tells us the truth, unless it is manipulated to indicate something else. Verbally we can say that it rains even if we have wonderful weather with a shining sun and blue sky. It is pretty easy: we fib or even worse, we lie.

If somebody is cold, then he will start to protect his body. Through shivering, folding his arms across his chest, or rubbing his hands, he will create heat. If we see somebody doing this, then we can expect that this person is cold. He is not faking.

Most nonverbal communication therefore comes from inside. Some bodily reactions such as growing and pupil dilatation cannot be influenced.

We conclude: If the body language of our counterparty is unconscious, we can expect that it is honest and real.

Suggestions for analyzing body language

As an acknowledgement: We are not able to say that all circumstances are the same. The reason simply is that every situation is different and everybody also reacts differently.

We do not need to be scared off or hope that we can analyze or judge someone just because of his body language.

If we add the spoken words, it may be possible for some specialists, but for the ordinary and average human beings, what is important is that we can just analyze and judge certain behaviors.

We always should have in mind that we are human and that means that we can also misinterpret situations.

133

Additionally, it is impossible to just take a small section of human behavior and use it as a sample to draw absolute conclusions for all human behavior.

To draw that conclusion, the interaction of all muscles within the human body is too complex.

Just imagine you want to drink a sip of water out of a glass on your desk. It is impossible to just take the water glass without making sure with your eyes where exactly the glass is situated on your desk.

As you pick up the water glass you will control the action through your eyes. That means that the motor function of your hand and the movement of your eyes work together.

In order to put these two actions into practice we will absorb, process, and analyze them all at the same time. If we just look at the eyes we cannot know that the hand picked up a glass.

Also when we move the hand with the glass to our mouth another reaction happens in our brain and our mouth: we can observe the movement of our lips.

Finally, we need to open our mouth a little bit so we can put the glass to our lips to drink.

We can imagine the never-ending interaction between our senses and body parts as well as the use of devices or the surrounding area that might be in order to achieve successful goals.

And there are thousands of goals like that during an average day.

To unlock the secrets of body language we need to realize again and again the following guideline in order to avoid a wrong interpretation:

Body language can only be unlocked if the behavior symbolizes a reaction to an action!

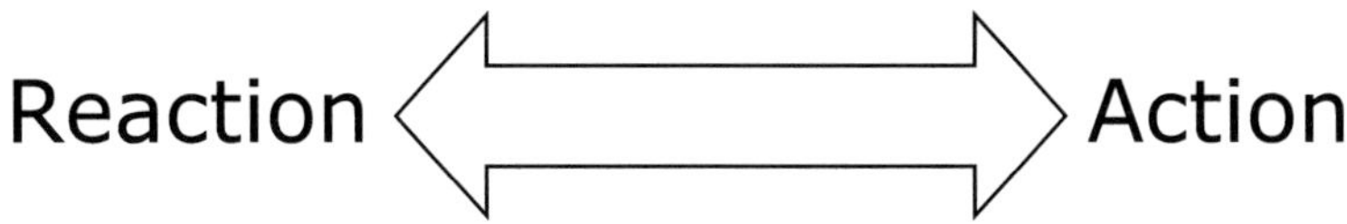

What does that mean? Well, we act by saying or doing something that others react to. Only at that moment it is possible to correctly interpret the reaction.

For example: Somebody with arms crossed in front of his chest sitting before us does not necessarily mean that he does not like us.

Maybe he is just not too keen on the new surrounding area; maybe he is cold or maybe he has a physical impairment so he has to sit like that.

It is impossible to have a definite analysis!

But: if we say or do something and then the other person crosses his arms in front of his chest we can be sure that it is a reaction to our action and it is possible to clearly analyze it!

Chapter 7 – From Word to Coherent Sentence

Words, words, words

> *"Men should use common words to say uncommon things."*
> **Arthur Schopenhauer, German philosopher**
> *(1788 - 1860)*

Word style

According to a 2002 report issued by the European Parliament, "10-20 percent of the Union's population and up to 30 percent of the population of EU candidate countries are unable to understand and use the printed and written matter necessary to function in society."

(http://www.dw-world.de/dw/article/0,2144,445044,00.html)

To take the German language as an example, it is estimated that the language contains 300,000 to 400,000 words.

The average German uses 12,000 to 16,000 German words and from 3,000 to 4,000 foreign words, but can understand four times as many words as he uses.

Are we forgetting how to speak? Here is a table showing how the use of words has changed on average in the past years.

While in 1965, an average of 1,756 words were in common usage in Germany, today the number is probably less than 1,318 different words.

Vocabulary use In Germany			
1965	average	1756	words
1975	average	1672	words
1985	average	1521	words
1995	average	1318	words

(Source: Society for the German Language. *General Anzeiger Bonn* newspaper, 1999)

What's also interesting is that 90% of spoken or written texts use the same 2,000 words. And only 4,000 words are needed to formulate 95% of texts. In English, nine different words account for 25% of usage.

Eight parts of speech

We can classify all words into 8 parts of speech:

Nouns	presentation, speech	Preposition	from, to
Pronouns	he, she	Conjunction	and, if
Adjectives	two, success-ful	Adverbs	often, only
Verbs	to speak, to be	Interjections	Oh

138

But language does not exist just out of incoherent words. It is influenced through:

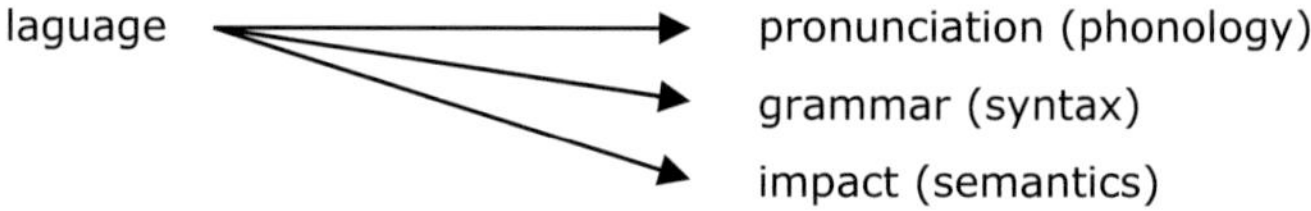

The affective resonance of a word

By the affective resonance of a word we mean people's emotional reaction to it. The author did a survey of approximately 200 people from different age-groups who should sort the following (randomly) fictitious names for candy. The result is as follows (in percent):

	Sweet	Salty	Bitter	Sour
Bumpies	6,82	3,41	14,20	75,57
Checkies	29,44	9,44	23,33	37,78
Quellies	11,24	9,55	32,02	47,19
Abaray	15,70	47,09	14,53	22,67
Sassos	51,18	9,41	25,29	14,12

The table shows that more than 75 % of the respondents gave the (fictitious) word 'bumpies' the flavor 'sweet', and 47 % of the respondents gave the word 'abaray' the flavor 'bitter'.

It is clearly demonstrated that different words create different feelings for people. Additionally, the survey asked what kind of a food (candy) the fictitious word might stand for. The results (excerpt) are as follows:

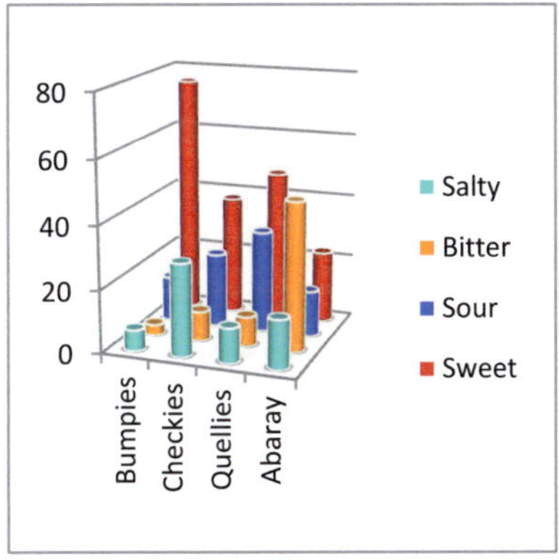

	Bumpies	Checkies	Quellies	Abaray	Sassos
chewing gum	21,05	10,87	18,09	4,41	
wine gums	10,53	14,13	29,79	7,35	6,80
gummi bear candy	12,63	8,70	11,70		3,88
licorice		4,35	1,06	27,94	25,24
hard candy	29,47	17,39	18,09	14,71	21,36
marshmallows	4,21		8,51	1,47	
fizzy tablet		1,09	8,51		
chocolate	6,32	14,13	1,06	30,88	2,91
cracker	8,42	10,87	1,06	5,88	
chips	7,37	15,22	1,06	2,94	23,30
pretzel sticks		3,26	1,06		10,68
Turkish cookies				4,41	
tacos					5,83

In 2001, the author asked about 160 students to estimate the affective (emotional) resonance of the ten words listed below. The shaded fields indicate the most frequent associations made. It's clear to see that words generate particular feelings in readers or listeners.

On the left are the following associations: On the right, these associations:

unpleasant...	...pleasant
cold...	...warm
angular...	...round
rough...	...smooth
old...	...new

actually

unpleasant...	16	27	44	18	27	14	4	3	5	...pleasant
cold...	4	23	29	27	38	12	11	9	3	...warm
angular...	11	25	30	20	29	16	14	9	4	...round
rough...	5	14	27	24	33	13	20	18	3	...smooth
old...	6	23	28	15	56	12	11	5	0	...new

Cologne

unpleasant...	1	1	2	4	10	13	44	32	52	...pleasant
cold...	9	9	15	9	19	24	26	23	25	...warm
angular...	7	9	16	15	24	20	36	15	17	...round
rough...	3	8	11	20	40	29	26	14	8	...smooth
old...	27	19	21	7	37	15	13	15	6	...new

war

unpleasant...	125	20	7	1	1	0	0	1	1	...pleasant
cold...	118	24	7	3	4	0	0	0	1	...warm
angular...	85	31	18	8	9	3	3	0	1	...round
rough...	125	15	7	4	3	0	2	0	2	...smooth
old...	80	7	20	11	26	4	4	2	3	...new

spontaneous

unpleasant...	0	1	0	2	10	21	36	44	45	...pleasant
cold...	2	2	4	7	27	30	46	28	12	...warm
angular...	4	11	17	11	28	15	37	24	9	...round
rough...	2	5	15	18	31	37	28	16	6	...smooth
old...	1	4	1	4	26	22	33	36	30	...new

self-assured

unpleasant...	0	1	1	2	8	11	48	45	41	...pleasant
cold...	3	4	11	20	29	19	33	22	15	...warm
angular...	3	10	20	19	28	19	28	12	16	...round
rough...	2	6	17	30	34	20	19	15	14	...smooth
old...	4	1	6	10	71	28	21	12	6	...new

only

unpleasant...	15	33	31	25	30	9	9	2	3	...pleasant
cold...	12	26	33	35	31	9	6	1	1	...warm
angular...	10	21	20	24	27	16	22	10	5	...round
rough...	6	15	25	36	30	15	15	9	4	...smooth
old...	14	13	17	22	63	14	9	3	0	...new

thank you

unpleasant...	0	0	1	0	2	4	16	45	87	...pleasant
cold...	1	1	0	0	3	6	23	45	75	...warm
angular...	1	0	3	4	11	8	37	40	52	...round
rough...	2	0	0	6	18	19	35	43	33	...smooth
old...	18	12	11	11	65	14	12	8	4	...new

success

unpleasant...	0	0	0	0	5	6	20	55	70	...pleasant
cold...	2	6	12	4	23	24	28	22	34	...warm
angular...	6	8	11	11	17	33	27	20	23	...round
rough...	4	11	8	12	35	20	24	23	18	...smooth
old...	4	3	7	7	58	19	19	23	17	...new

interesting

unpleasant...	0	1	3	5	9	17	47	37	38	...pleasant
cold...	1	6	14	15	27	33	36	26	1	...warm
angular...	10	14	21	18	29	29	23	8	5	...round
rough...	2	14	29	25	33	23	17	9	7	...smooth
old...	5	12	15	11	26	15	19	20	34	...new

body odour

unpleasant...	62	31	13	7	26	10	2	4	3	...pleasant
cold...	10	12	18	8	22	23	28	18	19	...warm
angular...	10	10	19	19	37	30	18	10	6	...round
rough...	14	12	31	22	37	19	15	6	2	...smooth
old...	36	18	27	16	41	13	3	2	1	...new

Meaning relationships between lexemes

A lexeme is the fundamental unit of vocabulary of a language, for example, *find, finds, found* and *finding* are forms of the English lexeme *find*. In the following we will look at how words can be related to one another.

- Synonyms
    - are lexemes that mean the same thing.
        - building, edifice
    - Two lexemes may be synonymous in one sentence and not in another.
        - "The pencil is sharp."
        - "You're looking sharp today."
    - The lexeme 'sharp' has a different meaning in each case.

- Hyponyms
    - are lexemes subsumed under a generic term.
        - Woman is a hyponym of human.
        - Flower is a hyponym of plant.

- Cohyponyms
    - are lexemes that both fall under the same generic category.
        - Man, woman and child all belong to the category of human.

- Antonyms
    - are lexemes that mean the opposite. A distinction is made here between gradable, complementary and relational antonyms.
        - Gradable antonyms are two ends of a spectrum that can have various gradations, such as light - dark (very light - very dark)
        - Complementary antonyms express absolute opposites such as pregnant - not pregnant (Somewhat pregnant is not possible and hence not gradable.)

- Relational antonyms describe the same situation from opposite sides.

    o question - answer

- Incompatibility

    o represents something that is lexically irreconcilable. These are lexemes that are mutually exclusive.

        - Either the door is open or it is closed. (Both can't be true at the same time).

Lexeme groupings

Lexemes may form groups. We then say that they are part of 'collocations'. There are three ways to form collocations.

- predictably

    o for example, 'pig' and 'squeal'

        - "A pig …"

- variably

    o for example, 'talk' and interesting, boring, fascinating, long-winded, etc.'

        - "His talk was …"

- unpredictably

    o for example, 'have'

        - "… has …"

Lexemes with the same and different meaning

There are two groups here: polysemes and homonyms.

- A polyseme is a word with multiple related meanings.

    o for example, 'sharp' (a knife, a look, a photo, a contrast, hearing, criticism)

143

- Homonyms are lexemes that sound the same but are spelled differently, or lexemes that have two different meanings.

    - o for example 'nail' (can be either a metal pin or a fingernail)

Incidentally: when two lexemes are related, they are said to have a lexical relationship.

- "The <u>sentences</u> were skilfully formulated. He particularly liked the individual <u>words</u>."

144

'Actually' means 'actually not'

Of course, no word is inherently 'bad' or 'good'. But the choice of words (understandably) influences the listener.

Some words are automatically discarded as 'not good' (for example, 'odour'), while others produce a more pleasant effect (like the word 'scent').

Refer back to what we learned about the affective resonance of a word.

one	"One knows how difficult it is …" Who is 'one'? Are we speaking out here for anonymity? Better: "Those affected …" or "I …" or "New Yorkers …"
just	"Just look it up." Why just? Better: "Please look it up."
actually	"I actually find that good." But only actually. 'Actually' really means 'actually not'. The word 'actually' is meant to express a certain reservation; the speaker is leaving himself a way out. In most cases, the word 'actually' can simply be omitted. Better: "I find that good." An exception: 'It actually means'
somehow/sometime/somehow and similar words	"That somehow seems strange to me." Better: "That seems strange to me."

should/could/must	"You should do something about it." Should doesn't mean that the person in question will really do whatever it is.
	This apparently polite form is designed not to hurt anyone. But this does not serve the goal-orientated direction of a dialogue.
	Better: "Take care of this please."
simply	"Simply take a look at the documents." 'Simply' seems to signalize something quick and easy.
	Apparently, not much time is needed to look through these documents.
	Better: "Please take a look now at the documents."
well/so	"So, let's go on." The word 'so' at the beginning of a sentence seems to indicate that the next step in the logical structure of the dialogue will follow.
	But usually the sentence will have exactly the same meaning without this word.
	Better: "Let's go on …"

The Power of Words – Two countries divided by a common language

"Now that the age-old dream, which never materialized, of a universal language has evaporated, we note that English is in the process of becoming if not the universal at least an omnipresent language.

In many multilingual countries it has become the language of communication.

Globally it is imposing itself as the language of business, aviation and scientific research. Is this a pure benefit for humanity, or does it conceal risks or even dangers?

Is the spreading of English a secondary effect of Americanization? Is linguistic diversity being sacrificed? Only if the countries affected submit to linguistic and cultural homogenization.

The ideal - which remains within reach - would be to accept English as a practical tool of communication without ceasing to strive for the maintenance and strength of other languages in symbiosis with their own cultures."

Eva Kushner, 'English as Global Language: Problems, Dangers, Opportunities, 2003'

Don'ts

A good presentation doesn't need to resort to certain detrimental words or sounds. Therefore, avoid the following:

Vernacular	top dog, doormat, dicey, really?
Vague words	thing, stuff, nice, great
Archaic words	betwixt, hither, gay, merry
Hesitation words	you know, and so, well, naturally, you see
Abbreviations and acronyms. Exceptions	EU, USA
Hesitation sounds	um, uh, em
Youth slang	'Get it?' instead 'Do you understand? cool, mind blowing, awesome; boob tube for television

Foreign words and phrases	Expressions such as ad infinitum; ad nauseum; c'est la vie; crème de la crème; fait accompli; in loco parentis; je ne sais quoi; joie de vivre; mea culpa; mirabile dictu; modus vivendi; ne plus ultra; non compos mentis; par excellence; persona non grata; quid pro quo; raison d`être; sine qua non; très; verboten and vive la différence, though perfectly good foreign words and phrases, are, when used by English-speaking people, simply wearisome. If you do use them, translate them immediately! (Robert Hartwell Fiske, "The Dimwit's Dictionary", Marion Street Press, Inc., 2002)

149

Do's

Keep your language lively. Therefore, use:

- few nouns and plenty of verbs

  o Not: "the implementation", but "We implemented".

- Plenty of adjectives

  o Not: "the woman", but instead: "the good-looking woman with the sly smile".

From letters to scriptures – Forms of handwriting

Do we get irritated by the fact that sometimes we use capitalized letters and sometimes we use lower case?

Here is a small excursion to the different forms of script (Chirography).

majuscule	minuscule	Carolingian minuscule
in between 2 lines, without ascenders /decenders	up to 4 lines, with ascenders/decenders	dual alphabet
capital letters	lower case letters	combination of majuscule and minuscule
AB	bp	Ap
Greece: from 3rd century BC Rome: from 1st century AD	Greece: from 7th / 8th century AD	after Charles the Great (742 -814 AD)

Words just written with large scaled capitalized letters are called 'MAJUSCULE'. Words written in small scaled capital letter are called "minuscule"

In presentation different graphical extremes are distinguished. These are:

- italic type
- bold type
- color
- other accentuation

And then abbreviations again

It could be that we want to write as easily as possible. Every letter which needs to be written, costs time. Therefore: abbreviate?

- Truncate
  - means the replacement of some letters at the end of a word though a period or another punctuation mark. "min" = minimum
- contraction
  - to elide some letters within a word. do not = don't
- character
  - is a symbol that displays a word. ® = registered trademark

Phrasing / locution

- perlocutionary act =
  - the act of speaking with the intention of influencing the listener (e.g., effect on feelings, thoughts, and action of the listener.) It should have consequences for the listener.
- locutionary act =
  - the act of speaking with respect to articulation, structure, and logic of a statement
- illocutionary act =
  - the act of speaking with regards to its communicative function (e.g., appeal, question, etc.)

It seems to be

- seemingly (it only seems to be, meaning NO)
  - He seemed to be listening.
- apparently (apparently meaning YES)
  - Apparently, he was listening.

Words become sentences

Every single word influences the statement made by our sentences. What does the best sentence style look like?

- fluid

- in a conversational tone

- brief (an average of 7 words)

- active sentences (better than passive constructions)

- new thought - new sentence - only macro block (keep the point in mind)

Avoid:

- convoluted sentences

- changes of syntax within a sentence (anacoluthon)

Incidentally: It is better nowadays to misspeak once in awhile than to build sentence structures that hardly anyone can follow.

Counterfactual conditional sentence

A counterfactual conditional sentence is a conditional sentence that is always true because it starts from a false premise.

A premise is an antecedent / prerequisite for a logical conclusion. "If I hadn't happened to be in the room at the time, then I wouldn't have … today."

Rhetorically speaking, such a sentence is only useful if we want to build the subsequent discussion or presentation based on an assumption.

At the same time, we prevent anyone from doubting the correctness of our assumption. "Let's assume the Earth is round. Then …"

Misleading sentences

Did you know that they are holding elections these days in shopping centres? "I saw the woman who was elected mayor in the shopping mall.

"It's better to write: "When I was at the shopping mall, I saw the woman who was elected mayor."

Another example: "She wore a ribbon in her hair which was blue." Better: "She wore a blue ribbon in her hair."

Incidentally: How do you like this contradiction?: "The only truth there is, is that there is no truth."

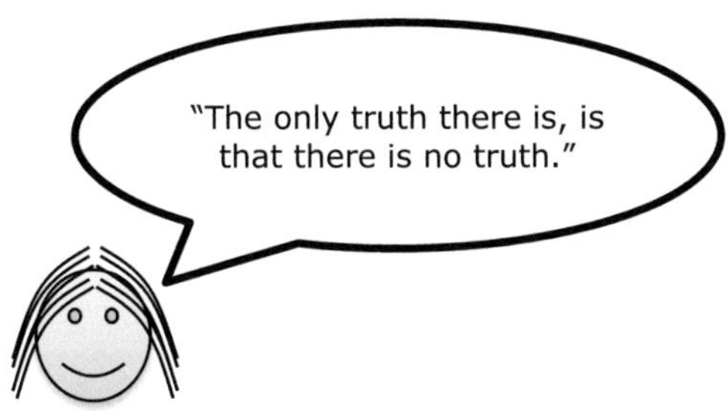

153

Clarification of verbal expressions

We always assume that we always want to communicate in a positive manner with others and therefore, we can draw conclusions from the words chosen or the design of the sentence structure.

Indeed, our own choice of words can be analyzed as well.

Interactive communication should bring clarification. Therefore we 'clarify' as follows:

Clarification of the meaning of single words

- If you speak a lot with substantives, then you indicate the status of a process

    o For example: "I've started." Clarification: ask yourself: "What exactly did you clarify or what are you supposed to clarify?"

    o We identify a process as a flow, a progression or construction. The status, on the other side, demonstrates the static point. In this case it seems to be difficult to work in a goal-oriented manner. If I accept a status for myself then I do not necessarily see the demand to change or adjust something. Typical words that indicate a part of a process are as follows:

        - impact
        - consignment
        - shipment
        - clearance

- Verbs, on the other hand, seem to clearly express what is meant:

    o for example: sleep, dream, fly, swim, stand, etc.

    o With a closer look we realize that verbs do not have to be distinct: negotiate, travel, dine, eat, etc.

    o Of course we do have an image of what we understand 'travel' to mean. But it is just an image. Therefore, our own image can vary from others. Misunderstandings are almost pre-programmed.

- Clarify the meaning of verbs.

    o for example: "I can clarify it." ask yourself: "What exactly do I want to clarify (until when, with whom, where, why, etc.)?"

- Clarify adjectives.

    o What do the following words mean to you: beautiful, nice, big, expensive, …? Is € 5 a lot or not much? For a bagel in a bakery obviously a lot, but for a luxury limousine, without doubt, relatively little. A dress which is nice in your eyes might be ugly to somebody else.

        ▪ for example: "That is an awesome deal!" Ask yourself how you (and how others) would define the word 'awesome'.

- In case of a comparative or superlative forms, you should clarify the meaning of words like more, bigger, further, better, and so on.

    o for example: "You just have to give me a better offer." Clarify: "Better than what?"

    o always, further, bigger, higher, faster seems to be the motto of our society. But what do we understand what the term 'further' should mean? Well, obviously further than before. But what exactly does that mean?

    o for example: "I believe that your offer is too expensive." Ask yourself: How do you define 'expensive' or 'too expensive' exactly?

        ▪ "More expensive than what?" or

        ▪ "Too expensive in comparison to what?"

- Clarify ellipsis

  o Don't we speak sometimes in riddles? "He said it." Who is 'he'? When did 'he' say it? Just through the ability of our brain to combine and complement information, people are able to put information together in a useful way. 'He' is supervisor Mertens. 'He' said something in a meeting yesterday. When the other persons perceives that differently (wrongly) then it can create misunderstandings.

  o for example: "I have communicated that." Ask yourself: "To whom did I communicate something, when, how, and why?"

- Clarify generalizations.

  o Generalizations are normally not true!

    - "I'm always so tired." Really 'always'? Day and night? Every minute of your life? Hard to believe, isn't it?

    - "Everybody did at some point ..." Really 'everybody'? Every native person of a pacific island, every Inuit in Greenland, every infant, every senior? Very questionable, isn't it?

    - "Never use a cellular phone in a church." Absolutely 'never'? What should you do in case of an accident, a catastrophe, or if you need to call for an ambulance ...? Far-fetched, isn't it?

  o For example: "I've never heard a decent suggestion from you." Ask: "Truly never?"

    - What do you think accounts for a decent suggestion from your point of view?

    - Does the person asking know how you perceive a decent suggestion?

    - Does he know that you expect to offer such a suggestion?

In the second step we should consider a complex (complex = comprehensive, recapitulate) conversation.

In order to be on the same track during the dialog we should always clarify our understanding with the other person.

- Clarify through recapitulation and summarization.

  - o Questions / you should ask:

    - "Up to now I understood the following"

    - "Did I understand right, that ..."

    - "Did you mean that ..."

    - "Is my interpretation right, that ..."

    - "Let me summarize what has been said. Please correct me, if I misunderstood something."

In case, the other person thought something different or combined it in a different way, now, in the development phase, is the opportunity to clarify misunderstandings.

157

Generalizations – "At one time or another, everyone has …"

Really everyone? Every single person on the planet …? "Well," you might say. "Of course, not <u>everyone</u> - but <u>almost</u> everyone."

Then I would reply: "Why don't you say <u>almost</u> everyone then?"

If you make generalizations, you run the risk that your statement will not apply to one of your listeners. This listener will then feel that he is being treated unfairly or even wrongfully.

Perhaps he will feel misunderstood or left out. Or even personally attacked. Is that what you want?

It is already a challenge to get your listeners on 'your side', to persuade them of the value of your ideas.

Why take the risk of creating one more 'enemy'?

Besides, most generalizations do not apply universally:

- "<u>Every</u> German learns English in school."

- "The British <u>all</u> love football."

- "<u>All</u> drivers are not careful enough in traffic."

- "I <u>always</u> get up at 7:00 in the morning."

- "<u>No one</u> speaks Chinese."

- "I <u>never</u> take medicine."

- "I would <u>never</u> do that."

- "<u>No one</u> would act that way.

There is a further risk entailed by the use of generalizations: "Every one of us, ladies and gentlemen, has had an experience with impolite young people." "Not me!", calls out one listener, indignant.

Can you imagine what kind of reaction this will prompt in your audience?

Can you picture how this kind of unexpected objection can completely distract you from what you were about to say?

You can avoid such unpleasantness by defusing any generalizations with a delimiting word:

- "<u>Almost</u> all of us have ..."
- "<u>Hardly</u> anyone would ..."
- "<u>Nearly</u> always (very frequently) ..."
- "<u>Virtually</u> no one ..."

Should your statement happen not to apply to one listener, this person will hardly feel personally singled out.

Because he might be the one who falls under <u>almost everyone</u>.

Tautology – doubled words

Tautologies or pleonasms are statements that are redundant. For example: a free gift. A gift is always free. That's why it is not necessary, and is even incorrect, to include the adjective 'free'.

old-age pensioner	me personally	simple and easy
Get off of me	cold ice	Could you repeat that again?
over and done with	plaid kilt	They mutually liked one another.
divide up	small dwarf	deep chasm
additional supplement	quiet whispering	free gift
one single	a new innovation	start again anew
false error	a knife-sharp cut	adequate enough
in this day and age	tuna fish	two twins
huge giant	lonely isolation	simple and easy
old-age pensioner	enormously huge	

Some tautologies are not immediately obvious:

once again	joint teamwork	a known fact
own initiative	controversial debate	severe devastation

at an early stage in time	new beginning	absolute silence
terrible catastrophe	return reply	

Tautology is the needless repetition of words or the complex description of a situation for lack of the proper word.

In medical terms, tautology can be caused by a disruption in normal language due to damage to the language centre of the brain (aphasia).

Clichés

Clichés are expressions that suffer from over-use.

poor as a beggar	dog-tired	naked as a jaybird
deadly earnest	rotten egg	filthy rich
pretty as a picture	dead as a doornail	bone-idle
bitter cold	ugly as sin	mad as a wet hen
blood red	as thick as they come	pitch-black
as dry as old bread	hot as hell	dumb as a fencepost
old as the hills	dirt cheap	dove grey
right on the money	smooth as silk	dead chic
sky-high		

Non-gradable adjectives

We often try to add gradations to adjectives that are actually absolutes. 'More unique' is impossible, because 'unique' is already 'unique'.

unemployed	ideal	ck
transparent	annually	stress-free
unequivocal	last (very last)	dead (dead as a doornail)
unique	square	cloudless (absolutely cloudless)
steely		

162 Cannibalism in the language?

"Lend me your ear."	"Give me your he-art."	"You caught my eye."
"You're pulling my leg."	"May I ask for your hand?"	

What the language describes – psyche and body

We can analyze our statements. Some statements provide us conclusions about a speaker's physical condition.

This is interesting if we can reach a possible medical impact. Here are some examples that are just a sample, and which are not medically comprehensive, and which should be used as indicators:

The following terms and definitions mean:	
kinaesthetic	Unconscious control of body movements
olfactory	Relating to the sense of smell
gustatory	Relating to the sense of taste
visual	Relating to the sense of sight
auditory	Relating to the sense of hearing
audio-visual	Relating to hearing and sight

Sense: gustatory

statement	releaser	possible consequence	approach
... I just lost my appetite ...	upcoming, expected, unpleasant situation	absence of appetite	danger of resignation, therefore, approach and dissolve situation

Sense: visual

statement	releaser	possible consequence	approach
... I cannot see that anymore	repeatedly negative seemingly behavior of other people	hypertension, sweating, roll the eyes	look for communication with the other person

Sense: olfactory

statement	releaser	possible consequence	approach
... that just stinks	longer, permanent, and recurring personal disturbances	nausea	implement practices for the subject anti-stress
... He just stinks ...	acquaintance with unappealing or ragged-seeming persons	itchiness, sneezing, runny nose, choking	seek to communicate with the other person

Sense: auditory

statement	releaser	possible consequence	approach
... I cannot hear that anymore	is hurt though words, hears something again and again	tinnitus, accurate hearing loss	"He doesn't mean it this way."

statement	releaser	possible consequence	approach
... I can't breathe	relict of disordered communication during childhood	asthma	therapy

Sense: kinaesthetic

statement	releaser	possible consequence	approach
... It makes my skin crawl	cannot get out of an embarrassing situation or out of a conflict	eczemas, psoriasis	Safety, to assist somebody, follow norms
... I'm going to puke	has aggravation, stress	stomach ache, diarrhea, gastric ulcer	anti-stress
... everything always falls on my shoulders	has lots of responsibility, excessive demand	neck-, shoulder-pain, herniated vertebral disk	learn how to say 'NO', work in a team, delegate work, massages
... that is a kick in the shins (back, or knee)	always feels excessive demand	hip- or knee-problems, herniated vertebral disk	anti-stress
... that worries me to death	e.g., lover's grief, critical, worries, problems	cardiac arrhythmia, tachycardia	strengthen your self-confidence
... I can't believe it	extraordinary experience	shock, trauma, chock, apathy	slowly draw into this or similar situation

Speak, say, talk

Our language is full of variety. Try to find synonyms (words that mean the same thing) for frequently used words to make your presentation more interesting.

Or find words that have a similar or stronger impact - depending on the statement you're trying to make. Your presentation will become more vivid and clear - and by all means more varied.

Example:

On the other hand, a different prefix added to the same word can some-times yield a completely different meaning.

up - load ⇔ up - river

down - load ⇔ down - river

pre - view ⇔ pre - serve

re - view ⇔ re - serve

The truth will out

167

The Effect of Our Voice on Listeners

Influence through the voice – suprasegmental traits

The following variations can influence how a statement is understood:

- pitch

    o rising pitch indicates a question and

    o falling pitch a statement.

- volume, or emphasis

- tempo

    o rapid speaking indicates urgency and

    o slow speaking seems more considered and emphatic

Pitch, volume and tempo come together to create the rhythm of the spoken language.

According to Dyckhoff / Westerhausen (Power Research Seminars, Bonn, 1999), our voice triggers the following reactions on the part of our listeners:

- Accelerated speech with a rigid rhythm:

    o Raises the listener's blood pressure, increases breathing and pulse frequency. The listener is at first attentive, but may become aggressive after a time.

- Wide range of vocal dynamics:

    o Increased rhythmical contractions of the skeletal musculature. The listener pays attention.

- Sharp articulation:

  - Pupils widen. The listener is in suspense and attentive.

- Strong rise and abrupt fall in pitch line:

  - Greater skin resistance, emotionalization. The listener feels directly addressed, may react defensively

- Staccato vocalization:

  - Increased stimulation of the nervous system. Listeners eventually become aggressive.

- Slow speaking without accentuated rhythms:

  - Blood pressure drops. Listeners' attention flags.

- Low range of vocal dynamics:

  - Breathing and pulse rates slow. Careful: listeners could fall asleep!

169

- Gentle, flowing speech melody:

  - Skeletal musculature relaxes. The listener is relaxed.

- Monotonous voice:

  - Narrowed pupils, low skin resistance, calming effect. Careful: listeners could fall asleep!

Our voice is at its best in a presentation when

- it is full and resonant,

- it can be heard clearly and distinctly,

- volume and speed vary.

The presenter

- pays attention to pitch and

- co-ordinates the rhythm of speech with his body language.

Paralinguistic traits

In addition to the above-mentioned options, there are also some additional tricks such as whispering.

Whispering can express a conspiratorial or secretive mood, but also indicates that something is being kept from a third party. Whispering is only in some cases suitable in a presentation.

It demands the full attention of listeners and should be used - if at all - only for a brief interlude, for example in order to make a situation clear.

In addition to whispering, this category also includes a hoarse or rough tone, a throaty or vibrating voice, for example when someone is about to cry.

170

Intonation as tool – semantic prosody

Finally, a few words on intonation. Semantic prosody refers to the way in which a sentence is spoken. Depending on how they are said, words may carry positive or negative associations:

Look at the following sentence and read it aloud:

- I'm working in the office today.

The main point made by the statement shifts depending on the emphasis placed on each word.

172 Always the same sentence - but five different emphases. Use intonation as a tool to make your presentation more 'colourful'.

Intonation also serves to

- raise the speaking tone

- strengthen the speaking tone

- stretch the speaking tone

Volume can also draw more attention to what you're saying. Even a spell of whispering can make listeners prick up their ears.

Caesura

Even wordless moments, deliberately inserted pauses, can grab the attention of your listeners and increase the suspense.

Pre-caesura:	• A deliberate delay - generates suspense.
Post-caesura:	• Pause after making a statement - gives listeners time to contemplate.

Pauses in speaking can serve for example …	• to clarify structure • to generate suspense • to (re)create calm • to compensate for rapid speaking • to catch your breath • to give participants a chance for the information to sink in.

173

Reading speed

Incidentally: Ideal speaking tempo is between 100 and 130 words a minute.

Reading speed can be calculated as follows: Number of words divided by seconds x 60 = words per minute (WpM)

< 100 WpM	←	extremely slow
100 – 150 WpM	—	slow
150 – 200 WpM	——	average
200 – 250 WpM	———	fast
> 250 WpM	———→	extremely fast

The act of speaking – function of language

The British philosopher John Langshag Austin (1911 – 1960) distinguished languages in the following functions (speech theory):

locutionary act:	• I Easy pronunciation of the words. • Count the words as such. • The content is described clearly.
perlocutionary act:	• Though the spoken words the success of its intension is worked towards. • For example, expectation, escape, or strategy.
illocutionary act:	• Accentuated pronunciation of the words. Here, for example, as a threat. • The words are used combative manner. • For example, promise, threat, or announcement.

Chapter 8 – Communicating with All Your Senses – and through Body Language

The Listeners Arrive

"What you look like determines how people look at you."
Carl Zuckmayer, German writer
(1896 - 1977)

The first impression

It only takes a maximum of seven seconds for someone to decide whether he likes the person he is looking at or not. Only seven seconds!

Frequently, much is riding on these seven seconds: making the sale, getting the job, or simply creating a positive atmosphere amongst the people who surround us at our jobs or in our private lives.

These seconds correspond with the first impression that the person opposite us has of us. We never get a second chance to make a first impression! This is why these seven seconds are so extraordinarily important for us.

Business partners, customers and guests expect much more from today's employees than merely professional knowledge and skills. The personal touch is increasingly in demand; interpersonal skills that are in step with the times often make the difference in making the deal.

Did you know that, in a job interview, the decision on whether to hire the candidate is made in the mind of the interviewer after only four minutes?

This shows us that the human component evidently has a very strong influence on the person we're speaking to.

First impressions can of course be deceiving. Perhaps the person is not really what he appears to be.

But what's important is that we have a maximum of seven seconds to make an impression.

175

And from our own point of view – subjectively – the first impression corresponds to reality.

In these first seconds, we have already judged the person to be sincere, self-conscious, friendly, self-assured, sales-oriented, etc.

How can we judge these qualities in so short a time? Perhaps the person hasn't even said anything yet! In other words, we would appear to react to things, elements, signals that are non-verbal.

You don't believe this? You would never pass judgment on someone after so short a time? Well, let's play a little game. In this game you are a travel agency employee.

The travel agency

Pretend you're sitting at your desk in a travel agency. It's not a very busy day. You're looking out the window.

Your travel agency is in a shopping arcade with a moderate amount of foot traffic. You can look out the large shop windows directly onto the arcade.

Suddenly you see a man - you would guess about 35 - running toward your travel agency. He seems to be in a hurry. His hair is tousled and in each hand he is holding a plastic grocery bag.

Behind him is a woman of about the same age pushing a stroller. With her other hand she is 'pulling' a small child behind her. The young man walks into your travel agency.

This is the end of the imaginary sequence.

Your task: Think about what kind of travel destination would appear to be suitable for this man (customer). Note down on a piece of paper a travel destination and give a brief reason for your choice.

<table>
<tr><td>travel destination:</td><td>brief reason:</td></tr>
<tr><td></td><td></td></tr>
</table>

Have you decided? In the seminars held by the author, the following answers are frequently given:

Majorca ...	• ..., because it's low-cost and not far away
The North or Baltic Sea ...	• ..., because they can be reached quickly.
A holiday on a farm ...	• ..., because of the children.

Many similar destinations are assumed. Have you also chosen this type of destination?

The question: What made you (and the participants in the author's seminars) choose this type of destination?

Answer: The man appears stressed, he needs some rest and relaxation, doesn't have much money (plastic grocery bags), and he has to find an inexpensive holiday because of the children.

Because of the children? Which children? "Well, there was the woman with the stroller and the child ..."

Was this woman actually with the man who has come into the travel agency? You can't be sure because the story didn't expressly say so.

But in our mind we form this picture, namely the picture of a man who is under stress, obviously doesn't have much money, who is probably a young father and is looking for a relaxing, stress-free holiday.

In our thoughts we already have a corresponding travel catalogue in our hands. But in reality it might be that this man really wants a catalogue of cruises for his mother who has just won a large sum of money in a sweepstakes.

Or who wants to blow through the life insurance money that has just been paid out to her.

If you reacted similarly to the seminar participants, this demonstrates that your first impression was formed based merely on a few details in the story. And it obviously happened in less than seven seconds.

Of course, we are only human and this is why we are susceptible to the power of the first impression - we aren't computers that react soberly and without emotion.

The risk of misinterpretation, however, means that we might get a false - possibly completely false - impression of a person. It follows that the ensuing sales pitch might not go off as well as it could.

The self-fulfilling prophecy

We all know about the effect called the 'self-fulfilling prophecy'. What is its significance here?

Imagine that our listeners get a positive first impression of us.

We have every reason to believe that our listener is a friendly, open person who displays interest in our presentation and has the necessary time and energy (and money) to watch us attentively and listen to what we have to say.

As partners in a dialogue, we both feel good about things, we feel mutual respect. We (and much more importantly - our listener) are already satisfied, without any sale (in the sense of the goal of the presentation) having been made.

And that is exceptionally important for us. The first impression was positive, perhaps even very positive. Our listener feels respected and has the impression that his needs will also be treated with the proper respect.

The 'self-fulfilling prophecy' is already at work. Namely: the listener expects - and is now certain - that the sales pitch (presentation) will be successful. To make it perfectly clear: 'all' we have done up until now is to build a positive first impression.

Isn't is great to be able to go home after doing our job, satisfied and pleased at the many nice participants / listeners we encountered today? But is this what the reality always looks like?

Haven't you sometimes gone home and complained about the nasty 'customers' with their never-ending special requests and contrary opinions?

No, this situation <u>can</u> happen sometimes but it should not be the rule. You have certainly heard people complain that service isn't what it used to be. Is there something to this?

Well, sometimes we might think so. Every one of us can contribute to creating a more positive service experience, however. And not only in terms of sales in shops, but also in selling our point of view in a presentation.

And it all starts with the first impression. If you face the day in a positive mood, if you value your listeners with all their needs, desires and questions, then you can bring much more harmony into your daily work.

The handmade jumper and the tie

Let's take a closer look at one of the aspects that goes into making a first impression: clothing.

Of course, each one of us is an individual and can in principle wear whatever suits us best. But not everyone we are dealing with will be able to see us from our best side if we are sitting opposite them wearing a lumpy handmade jumper and comfortable but unsightly footwear.

And not everyone will be able to see beyond our clothing if we appear all dressed up as if for a ball or the disco.

The people with whom we speak expect appropriate dress, in a style that is appropriate for our job, the product we are offering in our presentation, and naturally the location where the event is taking place.

Therefore, always be sure to choose a suitable outfit – and the door to success will open a little bit wider.

Welcoming the participants

Before an event begins (a seminar, conference, etc.), the presenter can greet the participants individually. It's up to you if you want to shake each participant's hand.

This is perhaps advisable with a smaller number of participants to create a personal atmosphere from the very start.

Please note: If you forget to personally greet anyone, you may have already created your first adversary or doubter! At the same time, you can use this opportunity to show your guests where to hang their coats, etc.

When there are more participants, or when you are introduced as speaker, you will then surely want to greet the group as a whole and avoid individual handshakes.

Greeting within the presentation

At the beginning of a presentation, the attendees should always be greeted. This catches their attention and creates a personal atmosphere.

When greeting your listeners, make eye contact and smile at them.

Introducing yourself

Introduce yourself (if your host or the organizer has not done so already). Three sensible variations are available:

most neutral and
fastest form

181

The last phrase might sound a bit abrupt. The modern norm is to give your first and last name. It's up to you whether you want to include any academic titles.

Leading into the topic

Most speakers use the beginning of the presentation to lead in to their topic. For example, they give:

- Their reason for choosing the topic
- The goal of the presentation
- The boundaries of what is to be covered
- An overview of the structure
- A first formulation of the statement or assumption
- A remark on how they plan to proceed

How Does Communication Work?

"If the doors of perception were cleansed,
everything would appear as it is - infinite."
William Blake, British poet
(1757 - 1827)

Physical sensation

We constantly absorb vast amounts of information through our five senses.

Take a look around you and become aware of how much information you take in through your eyes alone.

Not only words, letters or numbers are vital for communication, but also so-called 'physical sensations'.

We perceive:

Images:	• I 'see' something. • For example, the person sitting opposite me.
Odours:	• I 'smell' something. • For example, the perfume or Eau de Toilette that the person opposite me uses.
Feelings:	• I feel something. There are two possibilities here: • I feel (physically) the pencil I'm writing with, or • I feel (emotionally) kindly disposed toward the person with whom I'm speaking.

Taste:	• I 'taste' something.
	• For example, the coffee that I am drinking during our conversation.
Sounds:	• I 'hear' something.
	• For example, the volume of the spoken words.

From the above, we can already discern that our brain obviously does not store mere letters or data alone, but rather complex images (or films), images in which something is moving, in which sounds can be heard, that contain colours that affect our mood, and so forth.

We call these complex images 'sensations'. Our ultra-short-term memory perceives these sensations.

Encoding

Over time, sensations will be placed in the order of their significance. This process is called 'encoding'.

Its meaning on the other hand can be sorted out only if we can refer to earlier experiences and knowledge.

We define an 'object', that is in between four and five meters long, approximately 1.6 meters high, and 1.4 meters wide, mostly made out of colored metal, and which moves with four wheels in traffic, as a car.

Engineers of car manufacturers develop new models every year. When we see such new model for the first time on the street it is easy for our brain to define this new construction immediately as a car because of our memorized knowledge.

Our language works in a similar way.

Most people wrinkle their nose when they hear the expression 'body odor' and have their own interpretation of that expression (alternatively, the 'pictures' associated with it, first negative and unpleasant; they link this expression with their vision of perspiration, halitosis, and so on).

On the other hand, body odor is something natural. An infant can identify his mother through her smell.

Everybody seems to have his own typically scent. (Consider the bestseller by Patrick Süskind: 'Perfume: The Story of a Murderer'. In this book a person describes his life without having his own body odor.)

How would you evaluate the word 'scent'? Certainly positive, right? It is just one <u>word</u>, which is put together just out of five letters.

Nevertheless, these letters give it a value. Maybe, as you read this paragraph, some terms come to mind, which have a pleasant scent (blossom, coffee, food, perfume, etc.)?

185

The effect of colours – a brief psychology of colour

The effects of colour listed below apply primarily to Western culture.

Black

A magician often wears black. He doesn't give away all his secrets.

Black clothing makes the person opposite us seem to have something 'up his sleeve' (like a magician) that he is not telling us.

Since it doesn't reveal it all, i.e. has a secretive, enigmatic air, black business dress is acceptable only in some fields (such as design, media, etc.).

On the other hand, black also looks sophisticated, such as in eveningwear.

Makes an unpleasant impression on many people middle-aged and older because of its association with death and mourning.

Conveys a feeling of strength and power, as if the wearer were not prepared to get into a discussion.

White

In our culture, white stands for innocence, purity, cleanliness.

White clothing makes the person opposite us seem clean and 'innocent'.

But it also signalizes that the person is a 'blank page', meaning he doesn't know much about his material.

White in combination with another colour has a pleasant effect on many people.

Grey

A synonym for 'mousy'.

Grey clothing makes the person opposite us seem like someone who is hard-working but would rather stay in the background, unnoticed.

Is a popular choice of wardrobe colour for consultants or translators / interpreters.

Seems unobtrusive, discreet.

Preserves a feeling of distance.

Does not stimulate people to take action. Is therefore not used often in advertising or sales.

Grey in combination with black or white can produce interesting gradations.

If you like, try to analyse various TV commercials or advertisements according to these colour moods. You will be amazed how advertisers deliberately work with the psychological effects of colour.

Red

Signifies warmth, fondness, love, but also energy, assertiveness, movement, vitality.

Might provoke in us feelings of aggression, rebellion, even the desire for a 'revolution'.

Can make blood pressure rise.

Can cause our heart to beat faster and the pace of breathing to increase.

Red clothing makes the person opposite us seem impulsive – acting based on 'gut feelings', spontaneously. We assume that he is assertive and perhaps sometimes puts his foot down. Red can thus appear too aggressive – and hence can have a negative affect on a sales pitch.

187

Orange

Is regarded as a life-affirming colour.

Stands for cheerfulness and vitality.

Conveys readiness to communicate.

Leaves the impression that the information provided is superficial.

Is rarely found in business dress. (Cheerfulness and business are presumably not closely related?) Can form interesting combinations with other colours (for example, black).

Violet

Signalizes the need to drive others, to persuade and inspire.

Sometimes interpreted as emotionally immature.

Sometimes associated with non-conformist sexuality.

Supposedly worn by people experiencing a mid-life crisis.

Is rarely found in business dress.

Yellow

Is often used as a signal colour. Stands for freshness and power.

Conveys optimism, positive thinking.

Has a cheering effect and enhances communication.

Supports thinking and intellectual activities.

Yellow clothing makes the person opposite us seem to be trying to attract attention. "Hey, here I am!" Can sometimes appear slightly pushy.

Chapter 8 – Communicating with All Your Senses

Blue

Signifies to many people coolness, freshness, vastness.

Has a calming, dampening, affirmative effect on most people.

Relaxes the muscles.

Leaves the impression that the information provided is correct.

Blue clothing makes the person opposite us seem respectable. We can trust what this person says to us. This is why the colour blue is found very frequently in business dress.

Blue is many people's favourite colour.

Blue is a colour much favoured in uniforms and work clothes

Brown

Is the colour of many stimulants, such as chocolate, coffee, tobacco, etc.

Shows the desire to be close to the earth. Conveys a longing for security, warmth and affection.

Except for in fashionable (autumn) clothing colours, rarely found in business dress.

Green

People say that "green is a symbol for hope". This is why this colour exudes optimism for many people.

Green signifies nature, the environment, humaneness.

Green clothing makes the person opposite us seem like a 'nice' person, who does not necessarily act in a goal-oriented fashion. This is why green is rarely found in business dress.

Is this because humaneness is not a valued quality in working life?

Green catches attention.

Green increases concentration.

The Five Senses

How does appealing to the five senses help us to store more vivid images? People always complain that they can't remember information. They often think that information consists purely of numbers or letters.

Let's do an exercise with an imaginary banana. After reading through the following five sentences, sit down in a comfortable position, close your eyes and go through the instructions in your head:

- Close your eyes and imagine a banana. Try to see the banana with closed eyes. If you are able to do so, your sense of sight has been activated.

- Reach out and touch the banana with your eyes still closed. Feel the banana. If you are able to do so, your sense of touch has been activated.

- Pretend to put the banana up to your ear. Peel the banana. Do you hear the 'snap' of the peel opening? If you are able to do so, your sense of hearing has been activated.

- Put the peeled banana up to your nose. Can you smell it? If you are able to do so, your sense of smell has been activated.

- Now pretend that you're biting off a piece of banana. Try to taste it. If you are able to do so, your sense of taste has been activated.

With this exercise, we've shown you that 'banana' is not something we store in our memory as mere letters, but also in images.

And what is also important: with the help of our senses. The more vivid the images are, the more explicitly the senses have been addressed, and the better the information will be anchored in our mind.

What bearing does all this have on our presentation? It's best to speak in images as much as possible to make sure that listeners understand you and remember what you've said.

By paying attention to language, gestures, facial expressions, eye positions, etc. it is even possible to discern the different channels each of us tends to favour.

We remember information differently depending on how we have taken it in.

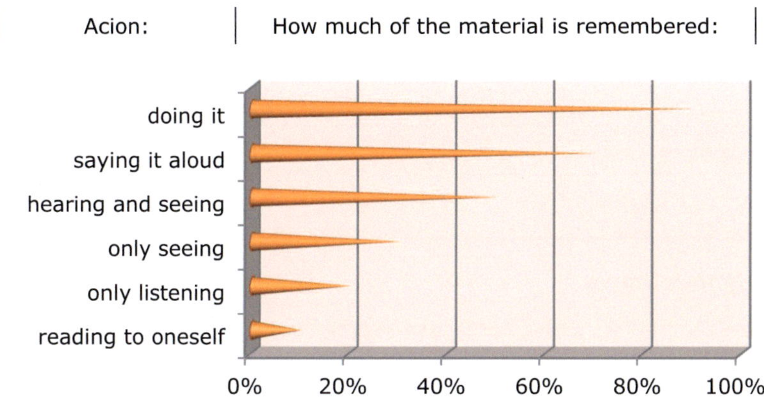

As you can see, actually doing something ourselves helps us to 'grasp' the material better.

Each person perceives his environment more or less intensely through the various channels.

The trick is to recognize what these preferred channels are and to use this information to adapt what we are saying to our listener's perceptual habits.

191

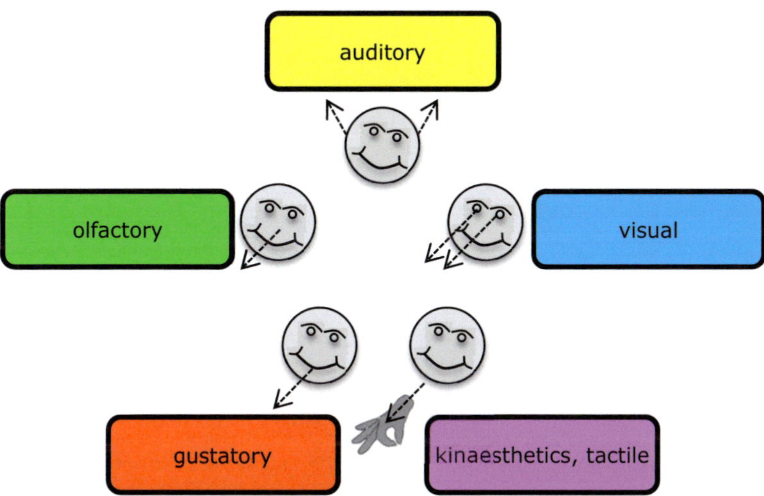

Touch	haptics	kinaesthetics, tactile
Smell	olfaction	olfactory
Taste	gusto	gustatory
Sight	optics	visual
Hearing	acoustics	auditory

Synaesthesia

Incidentally: As a rule, at least two senses are stimulated at a time. This is known as synaesthesia. In this case, several sensory impressions are melded together when the experience is put into words.

Moving images

As we have learned, the human brain processes images/films rather than material made up only of numbers and letters. Take advantage of this natural capacity by incorporating vivid images (or moving images = films) into your presentation.

Have your participants imagine something. Stimulating their imaginations will make it that much easier for you to teach them something. Travel agents might use the following strategy to sell a trip, for example:

"You are on holiday, it is early morning, and you are strolling along the beach barefoot. The sun has come up and is mirrored in the gently swirling waves.

You here the whooshing noise as the waves break on the shore. It is a pleasant, calming sound. You go closer to the water, feeling its refreshing coolness on your feet. Your feet feel revitalized.

You walk on and feel the sun trying to generate a lovely warmth on your skin. You hear seagulls calling in the background and breathe in the fresh, salty sea air with great relish.

If you concentrate hard - can you taste the salt on your tongue?"

Subjective truth – Is there only one truth?

We encode a sensation - and the construction created out of that is a real object for us. We are talking here about 'subjective truth'.

For one person the smell of a perfume is pleasant and for somebody else it seems to be pushy.

Both smell is the same scent but different people interpret it different. Each of them defined his own sense of (subjective) truth.

The truth of one individual does not necessarily conform to the truth of somebody else.

We even can assume that different individual truths can be extremely different from each other. ("I really think this dress is lovely!" - "I think it looks really ugly.")

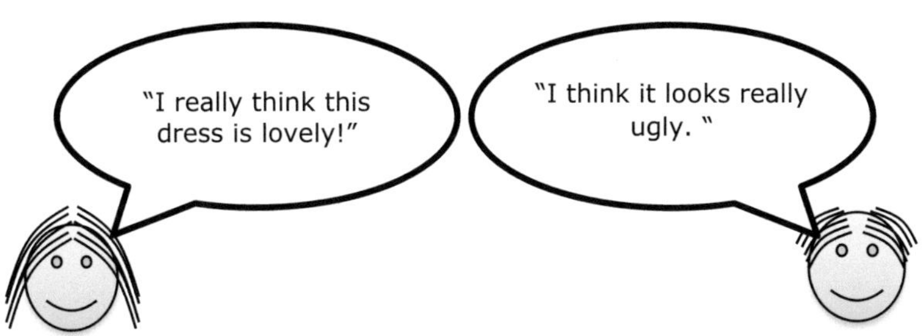

193

Storage

Ultimately, our construction is recognized in our long-term memory. It is memorized forever (we hope).

We communicate though our created memory of knowledge and experiences and our surroundings. The encoding drives our behavior.

Improvement and supplement

If we communicate with other people we recall our stored, encoded, physical sensations inside our brain.

Our pictures dictate our conversation. Unfortunately, we do not consider often enough the fact that these pictures might look completely different to the other person. Everybody has his <u>own</u> subjective truth.

When we listen to the words of other people there again is an encoding, some sort of a new-encoding, this time based on our experiences, therefore based on earlier cognition, impact, and word encoding.

What's aggravating is that we always leave out, deform, or generalize something in interpersonal communication. In fact on both sides.

In most cases it attracts nobody's attention. For almost every word spoken by others, we can insert our own definition.

Thereby a sense develops which we received - but that is our own interpretation - and it can vary significantly from what the other person wanted to say.

Otherwise, interpersonal communication would most likely not be possible.

Requirements of interpersonal communication

People need to, or rather want to, have or share something together.

Thereby the following terms and conditions of communication exist:

- rules
- standards
- values
- affiliation
- power

Basic principles of good communication

Do you want to communicate well? Than you should have the following in mind:

- communication is a matter of all senses

- communication helps to strengthen your social environment - "Do you want to talk about your presentation?"

- your audience or the other participants should possess the necessary strengths and skills

- in terms of communication, there are no wrong views or mistakes but only <u>different</u> views – just responses!

and so on:

- The more people who are addressed simultaneously (television), the less an individual person is addressed.

- The faster information is transmitted (e.g., telephone), the less time is for reconsideration.

The speech and body language at the podium

Extemporaneous speaking is not the same thing as holding a speech at a podium. Holding a speech begins not at the podium, but already when the speaker walks toward the podium.

The way there may seem quite long. The way the speaker stands up to give his talk can already influence the audience. Does he stand up hurriedly, or with seeming reluctance? Or does he exude self-confidence, looking calm, collected and natural?

Once having arrived at the podium, the speaker first takes a deep breath. This calms his nerves and allows him to collect his thoughts.

His weight is evenly distributed on both feet. The feet are positioned about hip wide apart. If the feet are too close together, the speaker gives the audience the impression of instability.

Movement during the presentation makes a more dynamic impact: bending forward signifies an active stance, while leaning back seemed more defensive. The speaker should stand up straight. If his head is held too high, though, he will immediately appear arrogant.

One mistake made by many beginners is to deliberately use certain gestures, facial expressions and body posture. The viewer will recognize at once that this is unnatural and put-on.

Every person has his own signature traits that make up his personality. The idea is not to distort these, because otherwise credibility will soon be forfeited.

Incidentally:

A survey conducted by the Association of German-Language Speechwriters (VRdS) of the 500 largest German companies, in which some 29,000 speeches are held annually, showed that:

about 90% of speeches are held for in-house listeners

about 10% of speeches are held before the public

And how long is a speech?

about 75% of the speeches are no longer than half an hour

about 13% of the speeches are less than 15 minutes

about 12% of the speeches are longer than an hour

(Source: G H I 4-02)

198

Chapter 9 – Selected Quotes

Quotes and Sayings

*"The quote, and especially the saying,
has other tasks as well:
It can serve as a kind of intellectual shorthand."*
**Ludwig Reiners, German writer
(1896 - 1957)**

It's good for uneducated people to read collections of quotesFehler! Textmarke nicht definiert.

These are supposedly the words of Sir Winston Churchill, who made many such quotable statements in his lifetime.

On the next few pages, the author has listed some quotes (and a few sayings), selected, of course, according to purely subjective considerations. This selection is not meant to target any particular reader.

The aim was rather to compile a small collection that might summon a smile or a chuckle. And naturally these quotes are suitable for use in a presentation.

I apologize if any errors have been made when the quotes were copied and translated for this book. I would very much appreciate it if you, dear reader, should notify me of any mistakes you might notice. Thank you for your help.

Famous quotes inspire us to contemplate, smile, or nod our heads in agreement. Some people react by saying: "Yes, isn't that so true?" or "How apt." In other words: your listeners will agree with most quotes.

This gives you the advantage of automatically creating a supportive mood. If you cite your source (<u>who</u> said it or wrote it), this adds further positive reinforcement to your argument ("Well, if Goethe / Adenauer / Jeanne d'Arc said it, then it must be true.").

199

If you can provide a year as well (<u>when</u> he / she said it ...), you underline how long this statement has already been accepted as fact. ("If Julius Caesar already said back in xx BC that ..., then this idea has been valid for a long, long time.")

This means that you should:

- Quote
    - word-for-word or
    - roughly rendered
    - translated
- Name your source
    - a person who is widely esteemed (not a dictator, for example!)
    - and who is known to most listeners (not your neighbour's grand-mother!)
- Give the year if possible
    - when the statement was made or
    - when the person lived whom you are quoting
- and if appropriate, the context in which the statement was made
    - Faust I
    - The Bible - New Testament
    - The New York Times
- Preface your quote with:
    - "Allow me to quote ..."
    - "A quote:"

Example:

- "Allow me to quote Joschka Fischer, who supposedly said, in my translation: 'People who have no idea what's going on can't possibly have an opinion.' End of quote."

Second example:

- "I would like to quote the following words by Charlie Chaplin, who once said: 'A day without laughter is a day wasted.'"

You can choose a telling quote as title for your presentation. But a quote can also be effective when used in your introduction, the main body of your talk or in the conclusion.

On the whole, speechmakers like to use quotes to lend greater credibility or respectability to their arguments. Utilize the advantage this brings you!

Tip for training: Pick out any quote. Use this quote to reinforce the impression made by your argument.

See the Appendix for some examples of quotes.

201

Abaelards, Peter 1079 - 1142	Know thyself!
Adenauer, Konrad 1876 - 1967	To think simply is a gift from God. To think simply and speak simply is a double gift from God.
	We all live under the same sky, but we don't all have the same horizon.
Aristotle 384 - 322 BC	No great genius is without a touch of madness.
Bible	... if any man will not work, neither let him eat. (Thessalonians 2, 3:10)
	Man does not live by bread alone ... (Matthew 4:4)
Blake, William 1757 - 1827	If the doors of perception were cleansed, everything would appear as it is - infinite.
Börne, Ludwig 1786 - 1837	We are ahead of the animals in some ways, but there is nothing in animals that is not also in us. (aphorism)
Brandt, Willy 1913 - 1992	Nothing happens by itself. And few things are lasting. (15 September 1992)
Brecht, Bertolt 1898 - 1956	First the grub, then the morals. (The Three-Penny Opera, 2nd Act, 2nd Finale)

Brillat-Savarin, Jean Anthelme 1755 - 1826	Tell me what you eat, and I'll tell you who you are. (Physiology of Taste)
Byron, Lord George Gordon, 1788 - 1824	The power of Thought is the magic of the Mind.
Canning, Georg 1770 - 1827	The whole art of speaking consists in knowing what not to say.
Cato, Marcus Portius 234 - 149 BC	Wise men learn more from fools than fools from the wise.
Cervantes, Miguel de 1547 - 1616	Misery is forgot, when there's something cooking in the pot. (Don Quixote)
Chaplin, Charlie 1889 - 1977	A day without laughter is a day wasted.
Chesterton, G.K. 1874 - 1936	Art consists of limitation. The most beautiful part of every picture is the frame.
Chevalier, Maurice 1888 - 1972	Millions long for immortality but do not know what to do with themselves on a rainy Sunday afternoon.
Christie, Agatha 1890 – 1976	Contentment is what we call the moment between two discontentments.
Churchill, Sir Winston 1874 - 1965	It's good for uneducated people to read collections of quotes.
	The only statistics you can trust are those you falsified yourself.
	A good speech should exhaust the topic, not the listeners.
Cicero, Marcus Tullius 106 - 43 BC	Liberae sunt nostrae cogitationes. (Our thoughts are free.)
Confucius 551 - 479 BC	A person with honeyed words and pious gestures is seldom a man of humanity.
Dali, Salvador 1909 - 1989	If you want to get people interested, you have to provoke them.
Dante Alighieri 1265 - 1321	The deed should be answer enough. (Divine Comedy)
Descartes, René 1596 - 1650	Cogito, ergo sum. (I think, therefore I am.) (Principia philosophiae - (Foundations of Philosophy)
Einstein, Albert 1879 - 1955	Imagination is more important than knowledge.
Eisenhower, Dwight David, 1890 - 1969	Motivation is the art of getting people to do what you want them to do because they want to do it.

Fellini, Federico 1920 - 1993	In marriage, the screenplay and direction come from the man, the dialogue and soundtrack from the woman.
Feuerbach, Ludwig 1804 - 1872	You are what you eat. (Natural Science and the Revolution)
Fontane, Theodor 1819 - 1898	A good aphorism is the wisdom of an entire book condensed into one sentence.
	The person who can only make his request with much trembling is instructive, because he in effect requests that his request be denied.
Ford, Henry 1883 - 1947	Coming together is a beginning, staying together is progress, and working together is success.
Freud, Sigmund 1856 - 1939	A human's sexual behaviour is often a model for his other reactions to the world. ("Civilized" Sexual Morality and Modern Nervousness)
	The first human who hurled an insult instead of a stone was the founder of civilization.
Frisch, Max 1911 - 1991	Dolphins are at least as intelligent as humans, but have no arms or hands; this is why they never conquered the world and why they are not destroying it.
Gaius Julius Caesar 100 - 47 BC	Veni, vidi, vici (I came, I saw, I conquered.)
Gandhi, Mohandas Karamchand Mahatma 1869 - 1948	Whatever you do may seem insignificant. but it is most important that you do it.
German Press Office 1996	Respect for the truth, the preservation of human dignity and the truthful informing of the public are the highest imperatives of the press. (Article 1)
Goethe, Johann Wolfgang von 1749 - 1832	If you want to talk, you have to have something to say. (to Friedrich von Müller, 16 August 1828)
	Enough words have been exchanged, / Now at last let me see some deeds! (Faust, 214)
	In the beginning was the deed! (Faust, 1237)
	It's not important that friends get together, but that they agree.

Goetz, Curt 1888 - 1960	Without imagination there would be no criminals and no poets. (Ingeborg)
Hauptmann, Gerhart 1862 - 1946	The eyes speak a more powerful language than the lips.
Hebbel, Christian Friedrich 1813 - 1863	The dog is man's sixth sense.
	Man is blind and merely dreams of seeing.
Hegel, Georg Friedrich Wilhelm 1770 - 1831	The ability to express everything in one's native language manifests a highly cultivated intellect and soul.
	Speech is thought given bodily form.
	The human only becomes human through education.
Heidegger, Martin 1889 - 1976	The memory is the assembly of thought.
Heine, Heinrich 1797 - 1856	Every era has its task, and by solving that task humanity progresses a step further.
Helvétius, Claude-Adrien 1715 - 1771	All that we are is what the things around us have made us. (Discourse on the Spirit of Man)
Hemingway, Ernest 1898 - 1961	The dignity of movement of an iceberg is due to only one-eighth of it being above water. (Death in the Afternoon, 1932)
	It takes two years to learn to talk, and fifty to learn to be silent.
Hesse, Hermann 1877 - 1962	Practice should be the result of contemplation, not vice versa.
Heuss, Theodor 1884 - 1963	One day machines will perhaps be able to think, but they will never have an imagination.
	But we Germans also have to think of the coming generation.
Hieronymus, Sophronius Eusebius around 347 - 420	He who excuses himself accuses himself.
Hugo, Victor 1802 - 1885	Laughter is the sun that drives winter from the human face.
Jaspers, Karl 1883 - 1969	The catastrophe that shook us did not destroy us. (1946)

Jünger, Ernst 1895 - 1998	If you think only in concepts and not images, you do the same injustice to the language as someone who thinks only in terms of social categories and not individuals.
Kant, Immanuel 1724 - 1804	Act as if the maxim of thy action were to become by thy will a universal law of nature. (Categorical Imperative, Critique of Practical Reason)
	Thinking is talking to yourself.
	Thoughts without content are empty, intuitions without concepts are blind.
Karajan, Herbert von 1908 - 1989	He who reaches all his goals has probably not set them high enough.
Kästner, Erich 1899 - 1974	Humans are good, it's only people that are bad.
Kennedy, John Fitzgerald 1917 - 1963	It's never too early to try, and it's never too late to talk.
Kierkegaard, Søren 1813 - 1855	The dead letter of writing often has much more influence than the living word.
King, Martin Luther 1929 - 1968	Success, recognition, and conformity are the bywords of the modern world where everyone seems to crave the anesthetizing security of being identified with the majority.
Lec, Stanislav Jerzy 1909 - 1966	It's not enough to speak to a topic, you have to speak to a person. (Undoctored Thoughts)
	From the smile at the corners of the mouth, the radius of freedom can be calculated.
	All that's remembered of most books are a few quotes. Why not just write quotes then?
Lessing, Gotthold Ephraim 1729 - 1781	You're a fast eater and a lazy walker. / Eat with your feet, my friend, and use your mouth for walking. (Sinngedichte)
	Absolute truth belongs to Thee alone.
Lucian 120 - 180	Six hours are enough for work; the others say to men: Live! (Sentences)
Lucretius, Titus Carus 97 - 55 BC	Nothing comes from nothing.

Luther, Martin 1483 - 1546	Why don't you farteth and burpeth? Didn't you fancy the meal?
Luxemburg, Rosa 1870 - 1919	Freedom is always and exclusively freedom for the one who thinks differently. (The Russian Revolution)
Mann, Thomas 1875 - 1955	I believe in the future of Germany. (10 October 1945)
Marcus Portius Cato 234 - 149 BC	Wise men learn more from fools than fools from the wise.
Matthöfer, Hans 1925 - 2009	Artificial intelligence is at any rate better than natural stupidity.
Maupassant, Guy de 1850 - 1893	It is the lives we encounter that make life worth living.
Montand, Yves 1921 - 1991	Women never lie. At the most, they invent the truth they happen to need at the moment.
Morgenstern, Christian 1871 - 1914	If you don't know your destination, you will never find the way there.
Nietzsche, Friedrich Wilhelm 1844 - 1900	In every real man a child is hiding that wants to play. It's up to you, dear women, to discover the child in man!
	Is not life a hundred times too short for us to bore ourselves?
	Talking about yourself all the time can also be a way of hiding.
Olivier, Sir Laurence 1907 - 1989	Conversation is the art of thinking of something important while saying something less important.
Orwell, George 1903 - 1950	Big Brother is watching you.
Perse, Saint-John 1887 - 1975	Diplomacy is the art of not saying with one hundred words what one could say with one.
Plato 427 - 348/347 BC	Learn to listen and you will even benefit from those who talk nonsense.
	Wisemen talk because they have something to say. Fools say something because they have to talk.
	Beginning is the most important part of work.
Protagoras 480 - 410 BC	Man is the measure of all things.

	There are two sides to every question.
Pulitzer, Joseph 1847 - 1911	Whatever you write: Put it before them briefly so they will read it, clearly so they will appreciate it, picturesquely so they will remember it and, above all, accurately so they will be guided by its light.
Reiners, Ludwig 1896 - 1957	The quote, and especially the saying, has other tasks as well: It can serve as a kind of intellectual shorthand.
Reuter, Ernst 1889 - 1953	We Germans have an enormous amount to make up for. (22.06.1945)
Reynolds, Sir Joshua 1723 - 1792	A room full of pictures is a room full of thoughts.
Rousseau, Jean-Jacques 1712 - 1778	Man is born free, but everywhere he is in chains. (The Social Contract)
Saint-Exupéry, Antoine de 1900 - 1944	Language is the source of misunderstandings.
	A smile is often the most essential thing. One is repaid by a smile. One is animated by a smile.
	It is only with the heart that one can see rightly; what is essential is invisible to the eye.
	All it takes to see clearly is to change the direction of one's gaze.
Schopenhauer, Arthur 1788 - 1860	Men should use common words to say uncommon things.
Seneca, Lucius Annaeus 4 BC - 45 AD	Let us say what we feel, and feel what we say. Let speech harmonize with life.
	Long is the road to learning by precepts, but short and successful by examples.
	Quod non vetat lex, hoc vetat fieri pudor. (Shame may restrain what law does not prohibit. Troades)
	Scientia potestas est. (Knowledge is power.)
	The more we absorb, the greater is our intellectual capacity.
Shakespeare, William 1564 - 1616	Saying doesn't make it so. (Othello)

	He thinks too much: such men are dangerous. (Julius Caesar)
	The rest is silence. (Hamlet)
Socrates 467/470 - 399 BC	We don't live to eat, but eat to live.
	I know nothing except the fact of my ignorance.
Stolz, Robert 1880 - 1975	If you fume about something one minute long, you lose 60 seconds of cheerfulness.
Swift, Jonathan 1667 - 1745	The best doctors in the world are Doctor Diet, Doctor Quiet and Doctor Merryman. (Polite Conversations)
Theodectes 380 - 340 BC	Rhetoric is the art of leading men by the power of speech to the conclusion desired by the orator.
Thomas Aquinas 1225(26) - 1274	Justice is spoiled in two ways: by the false cleverness of the wise and the violence of those in power.
Truffaut, François 1932 - 1984	Improvisation is when nobody notices that you prepared beforehand.
Truman, Harry S. 1884 - 1972	The flags of freedom fly over all Europe. (8 May 1945)
Tucholsky, Kurt 1890 - 1935	I looked at her and she returned my gaze: we caught each other's eye and took each other's hands.
Twain, Mark 1835 - 1910	Some German words are so long that they have a perspective. These things are not words, they are alphabetical processions.
	Kindness is the language that the deaf can hear and the blind can see.
Universal Declaration of Human Rights	All human beings are born free and equal in dignity and rights. They are endowed with reason and conscience and should act towards one another in a spirit of brotherhood. (Art. 1, 1948)
Ustinov, Sir Peter 1921 - 2004	The gentleman is a man who holds open the hotel door for his wife so she can carry the luggage inside.
	The last voice we will hear before the world explodes will be that of an expert telling us: This is technically impossible!

	Once there were many questions for which we had no answer. Today, in the computer age, there are many answers for which we don't yet have any questions.
	Everyone makes mistakes. The trick is to make them when no one is looking.
	If someone is shouting, his words are no longer important.
Vegesack, Siegfried von, 1888 - 1974	In the beginning was the word, but before the word was silence.
Watzlawick, Paul 1921 - 2007	Everyone thinks their reality is the true reality.
	You can't not communicate.
Wells, Herbert George 1815 - 1848	We have the complainers to thank for our progress. Satisfied people don't want to make a change.
Wilde, Oscar 1854 - 1900	To have been well brought up is a great drawback nowadays. It shuts one out from so much. (A Woman of No Importance)
	Progress is the realization of utopias. (The Soul of Man under Socialism)
	If you want to know what a woman really means – which, by the way, is always a dangerous thing to do – look at her, don't listen to her. (A Woman of No Importance)
	I never quarrel with actions. My one quarrel is with words. (The Picture of Dorian Gray)
	God, bless me with luxury. Necessities I can do without.
	Bigamy is having one wife too many. Monogamy is the same.
	A cynic is a man who knows the price of everything and the value of nothing. (The Picture of Dorian Gray)
	I always pass on good advice. It is the only thing to do with it. (An Ideal Husband)
	There is only one thing in the world worse than being talked about, and that is not being talked about.

	To expect the unexpected shows a thoroughly modern intellect.
Wolfe, Thomas Clayton [Tom] 1900 - 1938	Vanity is the attempt to flirt with yourself in a clouded mirror.
Zuckmayer, Carl 1896 - 1977	The easiest way to honour another person is to listen to him.
	What you look like determines how people look at you.
Zweig, Stefan 1881 - 1942	Freedom is not possible without authority (otherwise it would turn into chaos) – and authority is not possible without freedom (otherwise it would turn into tyranny).

Index

213

Editor and translator

Guido Michels is a self-employed management trainer and coach, certified interpreter and translator for English and French.

Furthermore, he is the Head of the Languages Department of the European University of Applied Sciences Rhine/Erft in Bruehl (EUFH), Germany and the Cologne Business School (CBS) in Cologne, Germany.

Both institutions offer BA programmes, CBS an MBA-programme as well.

Guido Michels holds in-house company training courses and open seminars on topics such as "Leadership", "Organisation and HR-Management", "Intercultural Competence" and "Intercultural Communication".

He frequently sets up intercultural seminars and training sessions for businesses and organisations all over Europe.

Contact: G.Michels@angel.de

12 Ratgeber in der kleinen Knigge-Reihe

Der kleine ... -Knigge [2100]

Anstands- und Banausen-...
Business- und Kunden-...
Büro- und Kollegen-...
Gäste- und Gastgeber-...
Gesellschafts- und Freunde-...
Outfit- und Stil-...
Interkulturelle- und
Auslands-...
Bewerbungs- und
Vorstellungs-...
Event- und Feste-...
Gastro- und Tischsitten-...
Speisen- und Exoten-...
Trinkkultur- und Getränke-...

Je 88 Seiten

Das kleine Handbuch der Rhetorik [2100]

Erfolgreich reden „Die Kunst, flott vorzutragen"
Körpersprache einsetzen „Mit Händen und Füßen sprechen"
Gezielt trainieren „Ich will endlich erfolgreich präsentieren!"
Nervosität austricksen „Mir zittern die Knie"
Begeistert überzeugen „Das rhetorische Feuer entfachen"
Unterschwellig manipulieren „Ich kriege dich schon!"
Wahrnehmung verzerren „Ich glaub' nur, was ich sehe."
Einwände entkräften „Das ist doch gar nicht machbar! – Oder doch?"
Gespräche führen „Zielorientierte und zeitsparende Gesprächslenkung"
Meetings leiten „Besprechungen erfolgreich führen"
Geschicktes Nudging „Das versteckte Anschubsen"
Interviews führen „Darf ich Sie mal fragen?"
Je 100 Seiten

Das Märchen der ...

professionellen Argumentation
harmlosen Fragen
sauberen Wahrheit
vertrauenswürdigen Fairness

... in der Rhetorik [2100]
Je 100 Seiten

4 Ratgeber in der Ego-Management-Reihe

Persönlichkeits-Management – Ego-Knigge 2100 Soft Skills, Selbst-Reflexion und Selbst-Bewusstsein

Stress-Management – Ego-Knigge 2100 Lampenfieber, Stressoren, Gerüchte, Mobbing, Burnout, Stressvermeidung

Zeit-Management – Ego-Knigge 2100 Umgang mit der Zeit, Organisation von Arbeitsabläufen, Perfektionismus, Zielsetzung

Gedächtnis-Management – Ego-Knigge 2100 Gehirn, Intelligenz, Schwachsinn – Hochbegabung, Gedächtnis, Lerntechniken.

Jeder Ratgeber 104 Seiten, A5, kartoniert

4 Ratgeber der Reihe Lebenseinstellung

Aberglauben-Knigge 2100 Von schwarzen Katzen, der linken Hand des Teufels und den Glücksbringern
Lügen- und Egoismus-Knigge 2100 Überleben durch Flunkern, Schummeln und Täuschen! Macht, Respekt, Wertschätzung? Lebenslüge und Lebensschutz
Glücks-Knigge 2100 Vom Glücklichsein, positiven Denken und von Freundschaften
Angst- und Optimismus-Knigge 2100 Die Furcht beherrschen, Ängste nutzen und positiv durchs Leben gehen.

Jeder Ratgeber 216 Seiten, A5, kartoniert

3 Ratgeber Bräutigam, Braut und Brautpaar

Bräutigam-Knigge 2100 Verlobung und Polterabend, Schwiegereltern und das Ja-Wort, Hochzeits-Outfit und Hochzeits-Kutsche

Braut-Knigge 2100 Brautkleid und Accessoires, Das große Hochzeitsfest, Höhepunkte und Hochzeitstanz

Brautpaar-Knigge 2100 Historisches und Sonderbares, Planung und Organisation, Aberglaube und Hochzeitsbräuche.

Jeder Ratgeber 104 Seiten, A5, kartoniert

3 Ratgeber Selbst-Coaching

Selbstbewusstsein Knigge 2100 Ich bin, ich kann, ich will. Das eigene Leben bestimmen, Soft Skills, The Winner 1.

Selbstwertgefühl Knigge 2100 Steh auf! Werde aktiv! Zeige Profil! Das eigene Leben beeinflussen, Motivation, The Winner 2.

Selbstoptimierung Knigge 2100 Optimistischer, attraktiver, authentischer. Das eigene Leben gestalten, Ansprüche, The Winner 3.

Jeder Ratgeber 120 Seiten, A5, kartoniert

Leben und Lifestyle

Adam allein auf der Welt Knigge [2100] Ein Buch mit Bildern vom ersten Menschen, seinen Gedanken und seiner Körpersprache, 104 Seiten, A5, ca. 155 Fotos

Jugend-Knigge [2100] Knigge für junge Leute und Berufseinsteiger, 152 Seiten

Alters-Knigge [2100] Abgehängt und abgeschoben? Altersdiskriminierung? Akzeptanz des Älterwerdens!, 152 Seiten

Zukunfts-Knigge [2100] Verfall der Sitten und Verlust der Wertschätzung? Umgangsformen in 100 Jahren. Zusammenleben mit Menschen, Maschinen und menschenähnlichen Robotern, 172 Seiten A5 kartoniert

KI-Knigge [2100] Leben mit der Künstlichen Intelligenz! Veränderungen im realen Umgang?, 196 Seiten A5 kartoniert

Wertschätzung-Knigge [2100] Gleichberechtigung, Gender und Respekt, Sexuelle Orientierung, Umgang bei Diskriminierung und Mobbing, 152 Seiten A5

Hochzeits-Knigge [2100] Hochzeitsbräuche, Geschenke, Brautjungfer, Trauung, Festgäste und Festmahl, 310 Seiten A5

Ü65- und Senioren-Knigge [2100] Die junge Alten und die alten Jungen, Kommunikation und Verständnis zwischen den Generationen, 180 Seiten A5

Blumen-Knigge [2100] Historisches, Mystisches, Festliches, Blumensprache, Umgang mit Blumen-Präsenten, 144 Seiten A5

Bekleidung! Ausdruck der Persönlichkeit – Lukas' Outfit-Knigge [2100], 196 Seiten A5

Nudel-Knigge [2100] Himmlische Teigwaren, 140 Seiten A5

Der Interkulturelle Kompetenz-Knigge [2100] Kultur, Kompetenz, Eindrücke – Gesten, Rituale, Zeitempfinden – Berichte, Tipps, Erlebnisse, 240 Seiten A5

China-Deutschland-Knigge [2100] Chinesen in Deutschland, 104 Seiten A5

Dschungel-Knigge [2100] Umgang in ungewohnter Umgebung, 192 Seiten A5

Von allen guten Geistern verlassen-Knigge [2100], 132 Seiten A5

Der Dicke-Knigge [2100] Aus dem prallen Leben des Dicken, 104 Seiten A5

Typisch Frau – Typisch Mann Knigge [2100] Unterschiede und Gemeinsamkeiten im Umgang mit dem anderen Geschlecht, 128 Seiten A5

Kulinarischer und Gastronomischer Knigge [2100] 284 Seiten A5

Klo- und Pinkel-Knigge [2100] Vom privaten und öffentlichen Bedürfnis - Umgangsformen im Tabu-Bereich, 104 Seiten A5

Alles hat seine Zeit-Knigge [2100] Umgang mit der Zeit, 294 Seite A5

Omi hüpf' mal Märchen meiner Großmutter, Erlebnisse ihre Jugend und wahre Geschichten meines Vaters von und über Omi Rickchen, Hardcover, 312 Seiten

Der Hunde-Knigge [2100] Umgang mit dem Hund – Hundesprache – Der Hund in der Gesellschaft, 180 Seiten A5

Welcome to Germany-Knigge [2100] Umgangsformen, Verhaltensmuster und gesellschaftliches Miteinander im deutschsprachigen Europa, 108 Seiten A5

Besuch willkommen Knigge [2100] Einladung, Gast, Geschenk, Empfang, Feier, Gastfreundschaft, 200 Seiten A5

Leben, Tod und Ansichten Austausch mit Berühmtheiten über Wichtiges und Unwichtiges im Leben, 116 Seiten A5

Last List Leid [2100] Verlogene Welt?, 160 Seiten A5

Mensch Macht Mörder [2100] Verfall der Umgangsformen?, 260 Seiten A5

Tod, Trauer, Totenkult-Knigge [2100] Sterben, Trost, Takt, Bestatten, Tradition, Vorsorge, Tabus, Vergänglichkeit und Sonderbares, 212 Seiten A5

Corona-Knigge [2100] Umgang mit dem Virus, 88 Seiten 12x19, kartoniert

Das kleine Knigge-Quiz [2100] 96 Seiten, 12x19 cm, kartoniert

Leben und Lifestyle

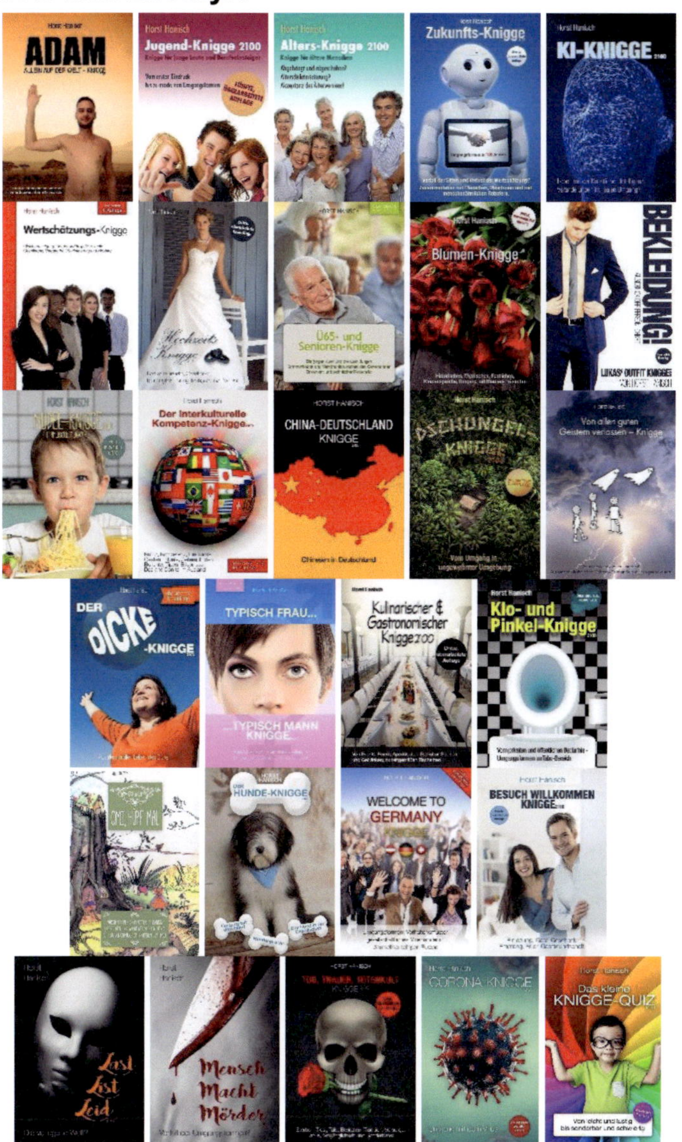

Rhetorik, Soft Skills, Hochschule, Beruf

Rhetorik ist Silber Von den ersten Schritten zu einer perfekten Präsentation, 336 Seiten A5, kartoniert, Zeichnungen

Moderation ist Gold Gesprächsführung, Umfragen, Talkrunden und Manipulation, 274 Seiten A5, kartoniert, Zeichnungen

Lebhafte Körpersprache in Vorträgen, Präsentationen, Gesprächen, 218 Seiten A5, kartoniert, ca. 290 Zeichnungen

Rhetoric – Mastering the Art of Persuasion, 222 Seiten A5, kartoniert

Discussion – Mastering the Skills of Moderation, 192 Seiten A5, kartoniert

Body Language in Europe, 196 Seiten A5, kartoniert, ca. 290 Zeichnungen

Das große Buch der Kommunikation und der Gesprächsführung [2100], 460 Seiten A5, kartoniert, Zeichnungen

Das große Buch der Rhetorik [2100] Tacheles reden; Präsentieren; manipulieren und überzeugen, 452 Seiten A5, kartoniert, viele Darstellungen

Trickreiche Rhetorik [2100] Psychologische Gesprächsführung, manipulierende Darstellung, unaufdringliches Nudging, 448 Seiten A5, kartoniert, Zeichnungen

Körpersprache [2100] **– Lüge, Verrat, Macht**, Im Beruf, vor Gericht, beim Flirt – Gewinnerpose und Demutshaltung; 440 Seiten A5, kartoniert, über 400 Zeichnungen

Soft Skills-Knigge [2100] Soziale, Persönlichkeit, Selbstmanagement, 480 Seiten A5, kartoniert, viele Darstellungen

Schlagfertigkeit-, Spontaneität-, Stegreif-Knigge [2100] Impulsiv handeln, verbale Angriffe kontern, Störungen entwaffnen, 104 Seiten A5

Pitch Skills und Überzeugungs-Knigge [2100] Elevator Pitch, Geldgeber beeindrucken, Feuer versprühen, 128 Seiten A5, kartoniert

Smalltalk-Knigge [2100] Vom kleinen Gespräch bis zum charmanten Flirt - Kontakt ausbauen, Sympathie zeigen, Begehrlichkeit wecken, 100 Seiten A5

Quassel-Knigge [2100] Quasseln, Quatschen, Quengeln oder Lebenswichtige Kommunikation – Gezielt eingesetzte Rhetorik – Aussagekräftiges Profil zeigen, 112 Seiten A5

Die moderne Führungskraft [2100] **Online und Präsenz,** Handbuch für souveräne Vorgesetzte und solche, die es werden wollen, 252 Seiten A5, kartoniert, Zeichnungen

Emotionale Rhetorik im Leben und rund um den Tod [2100] Vielfältige Kommunikation – Fiktiver Interview-Austausch mit Berühmtheiten, 260 Seiten A5

Innere Rhetorik [2100] Zielführende Kommunikation mit sich selbst, 140 Seiten A5

Kriegerische Rhetorik [2100] Sensible Diplomatie, einfühlsame Empathie, 156 Seiten A5

Blumige Rhetorik [2100] Zielführende Kommunikation mit sich selbst, 140 Seiten A5

Alles hat seine Zeit – Knigge [2100] Umgang mit der Zeit, 294 Seiten A5

Hochschul-Knigge [2100] Studentischer Umgang, 132 Seiten A5, kartoniert, Fotos

Jugend-Karriere-Knigge [2100] 224 Seiten A5, kartoniert, Zeichnungen, Checklisten

Bewerbungs-Knigge [2100] **für Frauen – Tina bewirbt sich / Bewerbungs-Knigge** [2100] **für Männer – Tom bewirbt sich**, Vorbereitung, Wahl der Kleidung, Verhalten beim Bewerbungsgespräch, je 128 Seiten A5, kartoniert, Fotos, Checklisten

Online-Bewerbungsgespräche-Knigge [2100] **Vorstellungsgespräche auf Distanz – Tina und Tom bewerben sich digital**, 128 Seiten A5, kartoniert, Zeichnungen

Kreativitäts-Knigge [2100], Visionärhaft denken, Scheuklappen sprengen, Mentales Risiko eingehen, 164 Seiten A5, kartoniert

Team und Typ-Knigge [2100], Ich und Wir, Typen und Charaktere, Team-Entwicklung, 128 Seiten A5, kartoniert, viele Darstellungen

Die flotte Generation Y im 21. Jahrhundert, selbstbewusst – lebensbetonend – flexibel,   116 Seiten A5, kartoniert, Zeichnungen

Die flotte Generation Z im 21. Jahrhundert, entscheidungsfreudig – effizient – eigenverantwortlich, 140 Seiten A5, kartoniert, Zeichnungen

Tele-Meeting [2100], Digitale Konferenz, Online-Unterricht, Homeoffice, 104 Seiten A5, kartoniert

Rhetorik, Soft Skills, Hochschule, Beruf

Englisch:

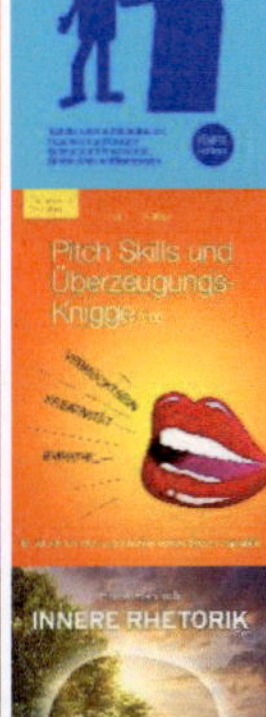

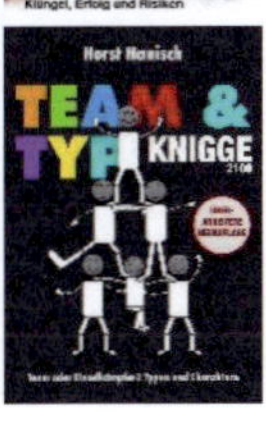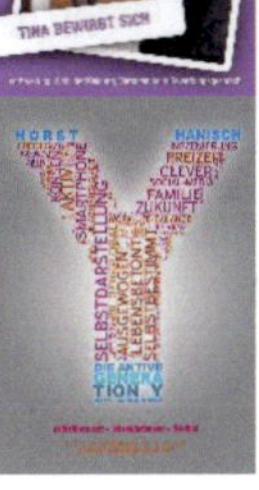

221

Beratung, Coaching, Seminar

Wer hat nicht gerne mit Menschen zu tun, die selbstbewusst und selbstsicher mit anderen Menschen umgehen?

Geschäftspartnern, die die elementaren Regeln des ‚Benimms' beherrschen, stehen die Türen zum Erfolg offen.

Unternehmen, die neben ihrer fachlichen Leistung auch ‚menschlich' überzeugen wollen, bieten wir für ihre Mitarbeiterinnen und Mitarbeiter aktives Training im Umgang mit Kunden, Gästen, Kollegen und Gesprächspartnern an.

Auf unserer Website informieren wir Sie über unsere Angebote:

- Firmen-Internes-Training
  → Business-Etikette und das Lehrmenü
  → Präsentieren, Moderieren, Kommunizieren
  → Körpersprache und ihre Geheimnisse
  → Teuflische Rhetorik und das Erkennen manipulativer Aspekte
  → Flottes Reden vor und zu anderen
  → Der erste entscheidende Eindruck
- Interkulturelles Training
  → Umgang mit Menschen anderer Kulturen
- Intensiv-Training für
  → TV-Auftritte
  → Vorträge
  → Präsentationen
  → Reden
- Fachliteratur und journalistische Beiträge
- Vorträge/Speaker
  → Vor kleinem und vor großem Publikum
- Workshops
  → Soft Skills
  → Team-Training

Individuelles Coaching für Einzelpersonen: Wer es ganz individuell mag, greift zurück auf ein Einzel-Coaching, auch als Online-Coaching. Hier werden ganz persönliche Herausforderungen angegangen, mit Themen wie:

- → Erscheinungsbild – Der Erste Eindruck
- → Selbstsicheres und authentisches Auftreten
- → Persönlichkeitsentfaltung
- → Bewerbungstraining
- → Rhetorik und Überzeugungskraft
- → Erfolgreiche Verhandlungsführung
- → Kommunikation und Konfliktbewältigung
- → Präsentations-Techniken und Moderation
- → Interkulturelle Kompetenz

und andere Themen – direkt auf die besonderen Bedürfnisse des Einzelnen zugeschnitten. Besuchen Sie uns auf www.knigge-seminare.de

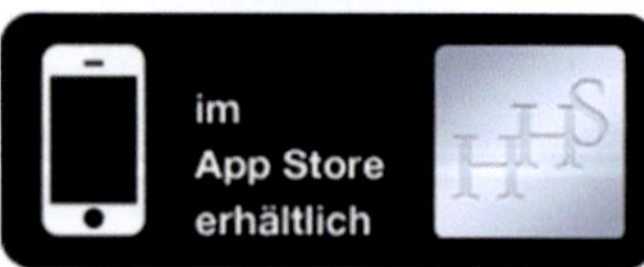